Kosher Patents

Kosher Patents

101 Ingenious Inventions To Help Jews Be Jewish

Adam L. Diament

Kosher Patents

101 Ingenious Inventions to Help Jews be Jewish

Adam L. Diament

aldgroups@gmail.com

Printed by CreateSpace

Cover illustrations licensed from iStockphoto®.

First Edition, 2016

Published in the United States of America

ISBN: 1522800077
ISBN-13: 978-1522800071

Dedication

To my wife Tiffany, daughters Joanna and Audrey, and
my parents Michael and Cynthia

Acknowledgments

A special thank you to the attorneys who have taken me under their wings throughout the years and have trained me in the art and science of law: Joseph Trojan, Michael Bolan, Neal Cohen, Jonathan Spangler, Rory Schermerhorn, Ronald Berman, and Judge Suzanne Segal. I would also like to thank my former intellectual property law professors: David McGowan, Adam Mossoff, and Lisa Ramsey. In addition, I would like to thank several rabbis who have been with me at various stages in my life: Rabbi Morton A. Wallack (Adat Shalom Synagogue), Rabbi Zevi Tenenbaum (Chabad of UC Irvine), and Rabbi Eli Rivkin (Chabad of Northridge). I would also like to thank the very helpful attorneys and staff at Trojan Law Offices: Dylan Dang, Francis Wong, Fredrick Tsang, Hee Jae Yoon, Michiko Speier and Rahil Ameripour.

Lastly, I would like to thank my editors: Nancy Dean, Cindy deRosier, Makan Mohageg, and Neal Cohen.

About The Author

Adam Louis Diament is a practicing patent attorney in Beverly Hills, California. Born in Memphis, Tennessee, he moved to California with his family when he was about one year old. He attended Adat Shalom Hebrew School and Los Angeles Hebrew High School for his Judaic studies, and Venice High School for his secular studies.

He earned a B.A. in *Religious Studies with an Emphasis in Judaism*, and *Molecular and Cell Biology with an Emphasis in Genetics* from the University of California, Berkeley, in 1997, a Ph.D. in *Genetics* from the University of California, Davis, in 2004, and a law degree from the University of San Diego School of Law in 2008. He lives in Los Angeles with his wife Tiffany and daughters Joanna and Audrey.

In his spare time (which he has little of), he enjoys family genealogy research, Lindy Hop swing dancing, playing with his kids, Scrabble, trivia games, and attempting to visit all 482 cities in California. He is the author of "The Top 10 Jewish...," a book of over 100 top-10 rankings of everything Jewish, available on Amazon.com.

Table of Contents

Introduction

What is a Patent?

Before explaining what *Kosher Patents* are, you should first have a general understanding of patents, the patent system, and Judaism. A patent is a right, granted by a government to an inventor, that allows the inventor to exclude others from manufacturing, using, or selling his or her invention.[1] If you make, use, or sell the patented invention without permission from the patent owner, then you can be sued for patent infringement.

The reason why governments grant patent rights is to encourage creativity and innovation. By granting inventors the right to exclude others from making their inventions, inventors can reap the financial rewards of their hard work without having to worry that someone else will freeload off their ideas. The theory is that when inventors are assured that no one else can legally copy their inventions, inventors are

---

[1] This book only deals with "utility patents," which are what most people think of when they think of patents. There are two other categories of patents in the United States, "design patents" and "plant patents." Design patents cover the intellectual property of the <u>look</u> of an object, but not any functional features. Plant patents are patents for asexually reproducing plants. Since this book focuses on inventions having functions, only utility patents are described. There are numerous design patents related to the design of Jewish items, but these are not included.

more willing to invest time, money, and resources into creating something new and useful for society.

Although the patent system was created to foster innovation, it does have its downsides. Once the government grants a patent, the inventor has a monopoly for that invention, and monopolies have the negative effect of higher prices for consumers. To balance the benefit of encouraging innovation against the cost to society for granting monopolies, the government has decided that patents rights can only last a limited amount of time (generally 20 years). After the 20-year period, the invention becomes part of the public domain and anyone may copy it freely.

How Do You Receive a Patent?

To receive a patent, an inventor must submit a patent application to a patent office. A patent application is generally drafted by a specialized attorney called a patent attorney. A patent attorney is required to have a background in science or engineering, and has extensive knowledge of the patent rules and regulations. The patent application consists of a detailed description of the invention and how it works. The application must also indicate what specific aspect of the invention deserves patent protection (in what are called "patent claims"). The patent claims must be for an invention that is not only "new," but also "useful," and "non-obvious" over what is already known.[2]

After submission to the patent office, a patent examiner will review the patent application by conducting a search for similar products and inventions. This search is called a "prior art" search. If the examiner agrees that the invention is new, useful, and non-obvious, then the patent office will grant the inventor a patent. If the examiner believes that the invention is

---

[2] The terms "new," "useful," and "non-obvious" are legal terms of art that are defined by statute and case law. Because new cases constantly arise, the definition of what constitutes a "new," "useful," and "non-obvious" invention is constantly developing.

not new, or perhaps is new, but is just an obvious extension of what is already known, then the patent office will reject the claims in the patent application.

When the claims of a patent application are rejected, the inventor has several options going forward. One option is to try to argue to the examiner that the rejection was improper. In this scenario, the inventor (or usually the patent attorney for the inventor) presents legal and factual arguments for the patentability of the invention, with the goal of convincing the examiner to change his or her mind.

Another option is to amend the patent claims so that the patent claims are not for a very broad invention, but for a narrow invention, because claims for a narrowly-tailored invention have a better chance of allowance than claims for a broad invention. For example, let's say you submit a patent application for a pencil and eraser combination where the pencil and eraser are connected together by a magnet. If you tried to claim that your invention was <u>all</u> pencil/eraser combinations, then your claim would easily be rejected because pencil/eraser combinations have been in existence for a long time. After a rejection, instead of fighting with the examiner to allow your pencil/eraser combination, you could amend your claim to limit your invention to the more specific pencil/eraser/magnet combination.[3] This combination would have a greater chance of allowance because it is narrower than your original claim for <u>any</u> pencil/eraser combination.

A third option after receiving a rejection is to do nothing. If you do nothing, your application will eventually become abandoned. You may want to abandon your patent application if you read the examiner's rejection and agree that what you originally thought was a new, useful, and non-obviousness invention, really wasn't that inventive after all.

---

[3] The claim for a pencil/eraser/magnet combination may also be rejected on obviousness grounds depending on what already exists in the prior art, but the example is merely an illustration of how one could amend a rejected broad claim into a narrower claim that might have a higher chance of allowance.

"How is that Patentable? It's So Stupid!"

When reading through some of the patents in this book, you might think a particular invention is the stupidest thing you've ever seen, and can't believe that the patent office would ever grant such a patent. Although the patent office does make mistakes, there is no "not-stupid" threshold in determining whether a patent should be granted. An invention may be stupid, but if it is new, useful, and not obvious, then the patent office should grant a patent for that invention.

Another reason that you might be puzzled about how a certain invention received a patent is that the invention may be much more nuanced than can be explained in a single paragraph in this book. To understand what actually was patented, you may have to read the full patent carefully. Almost all listed patents and patent applications in this book can be found using Google's patent search tool at http://www.google.com/patents by entering in the patent or patent application number in the patent search bar.

After reviewing thousands of patents for this book, the author believes that the patent office has been bamboozled into wrongly granting patents on more than a few occasions. The inventor's use of Jewish terminology for something plain and simple probably tricked a few unsuspecting patent examiners into thinking something was inventive, when in fact the only thing new was throwing in some Hebrew phrases into the patent application.

What Does Being Jewish Mean?

This is a question that has been asked and debated for hundreds of years. Is being Jewish like being part of an ethnic group or is faith required?

The short answer is that it is a little bit of both, and neither, all at the same time. Belief in the traditional tenants of the Jewish faith (such as belief in one G-d who created the universe) is not a requirement to be Jewish. An atheist Jew is just as much a Jew as a fully-practicing and believing Orthodox Jew. According to Jewish law, a person is Jewish if he or she was born to a Jewish mother, or converted to Judaism. In this respect, being Jewish is comparable to being an American citizen. You can be an American citizen by virtue of being born to American parents. It does not matter if you hold the most un-American beliefs, if you are born to American parents, your citizenship is generally automatic at birth. Similarly, a person is granted automatic Jewish "citizenship" at birth merely by being born to a Jewish mother.[4]

Becoming Jewish by converting is comparable to becoming a naturalized American citizen. To become a naturalized citizen, you must study, pass an exam, take an oath to give up all prior allegiances to other countries, and swear to uphold the laws and Constitution of the United States. Analogously, to convert to Judaism, you must study, renounce allegiances to other religions, and declare to uphold the practice of Jewish law.

Since faith is not required to be Jewish, and there is no single common Jewish ethnicity, what does it mean to be Jewish?[5] For Jews where observance and faith are not part of their lives, Judaism is primarily a culture. Culture may include participating in Jewish life cycle events, song, dance, food, having a Jewish social circle, celebrating holidays, having *Shabbat* dinners, and knowing a little bit of Hebrew.

---

[4] This is different from other religions, such as Christianity, where in order to be a Christian, faith in Jesus as the messiah is required. A person that does not hold this belief is not a Christian, even if born to Christian parents.

[5] There are many Jewish ethnic groups, such as Indian Jews, Ethiopian Jews, Persian Jews, European Jews, and Chinese Jews, to name a few. These communities have been around so long that they are ethnically indistinguishable from their non-Jewish community members, that is, Indian Jews look Indian, Ethiopian Jews look Ethiopian, Persian Jews look Persian, European Jews look European, and Chinese Jews look Chinese.

What is a Kosher Patent?

Now that you have a basic understanding of patents, the patent system, and what being Jewish means, what is a *Kosher Patent*? A *Kosher Patent* is not a formal government designation of a patent, but is a useful title the author has given to inventions that have been submitted to patent offices around the world that help Jewish people live a fuller, easier, and more joyful Jewish life. *Kosher Patents* have been grouped into one of eight categories, each category having a separate chapter. The *Kosher Patent* categories are:

(1) Holiday patents;
(2) Sacred text patents;
(3) *Shabbat* patents;
(4) *Kashrut* patents;
(5) Food and beverage patents;
(6) Garments and ritual item patents;
(7) Jewish time management patents; and,
(8) Miscellaneous patents.

Disclaimer

The purchase of this book does not constitute an attorney-client relationship. The contents of this book do not constitute legal advice (or Jewish observance advice) and should not be acted on as such. Many of the patents described are enforceable and you may be liable for patent infringement if you practice the patented invention without permission from the owner. Should you have any questions about practicing the described inventions, please consult a patent attorney.

* * *

Chapter 1
Holiday Patents

There's an old joke that goes, "The celebration of every Jewish holiday is the same: They tried to kill us, we won, let's eat." While the joke is a bit of an overstatement, there is some truth to it. There are around ten major Jewish holidays, depending on what you count as a major and minor holiday, and for at least four of them (*Sukkot*, *Hanukkah*, *Purim*, and *Pesach*) the joke applies. The following paragraphs briefly summarize the major Jewish holidays.

The Jewish New Year starts with *Rosh Hashanah* and usually occurs around September. *Rosh Hashanah* starts a ten-day period of reflection that ends with the holiday of *Yom Kippur*, the Day of Atonement. These two holidays are called "The High Holidays" and are so important that Jews who might not go to synagogue all year long attend *Rosh Hashanah* and *Yom Kippur* services. Jews who only go to synagogue just for these two holidays are commonly known as "Twice-a-Year Jews."

Shortly after *Yom Kippur*, around October, is *Sukkot*, which commemorates the Jews living in temporary huts as they left slavery in Egypt on their way to the Promised Land of Israel. At the end of *Sukkot* are two holidays, *Shmini Atzeret* and *Simchat Torah*, which commemorate the end of *Sukkot*, the end of the *Torah* reading cycle, and the beginning of the next *Torah* reading cycle.

Hanukkah, which occurs around December, is a celebration of the Jewish victory over the Seleucid Empire and rededication of the Jewish Holy Temple.[6]

Around March is the holiday of *Purim,* which celebrates Queen Esther's saving of the Jewish people from Haman's plot to kill the Jews of the Persian Empire.

In the spring is *Pesach* (Passover), which celebrates the Jewish people's liberation from Egyptian slavery. Around May is the holiday of *Shavuot,* which commemorates the day that G-d gave the Jewish people the *Torah.*[7] The last of the ten major holidays is *Tisha B'Av,* a solemn day of fasting that commemorates the destruction of both the First and Second Temple in Jerusalem.

Six of the eleven *Kosher Patents* relating to Jewish holidays are *Hanukkah* related, three relate to *Sukkot,* one for *Pesach,* and one for *Purim.*

---

[6] In today's Judaism, there are small synagogues or temples in each community. However, when Jews speak of the "Holy Temple" or "First Temple" or "Second Temple," they are referring to enormous temples that stood on the Temple Mount in Jerusalem and were considered the "House of G-d." The First Temple stood from 957 BCE to 586 BCE and the Second Temple stood from 515 BCE to 70 CE.

[7] There is a Jewish custom of not writing G-d's name where it may be erased or discarded, since it would be disrespectful to destroy G-d's name. Only holy scriptures have G-d's name fully written out. Even though traditionally this applied to writing G-d's name in Hebrew, in keeping with this same respect, many do not write G-d's name in English for the same reason.

Wand Activated Hanukkah Menorah

U.S. Patent Number: 6,053,622

Inventors: Victor Horowitz and James Boyd

Date Issued: April 24, 2000

Problem: *Hanukkah* commemorates a Jewish victory over the Seleucid Empire in 160 BCE. *Hanukkah* is celebrated for eight days to remember the miracle of sacred oil used in the Holy Temple that lasted for eight days (even though it was only supposed to last for one day). Although you must use an actual flame for lighting *Hanukkah* candles on a *menorah*, some people like to use an electric *menorah*.[8] Is there a way to light an electric *menorah* so that it looks like you are lighting a real *menorah*?

How the Problem is Solved: This electric *menorah* has a wand with a magnet in it. When the magnet of the wand is in proximity to one of the electric candles (an LED), it turns on only that one LED. As the wand moves from one LED to the next, each LED turns on, just as if you were using a candle to light the successive *Hanukkah* candles in order.

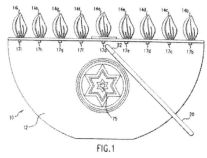

FIG.1

---

[8] A *menorah* is a seven-branched candelabrum and a *hanukkiah* is a nine-branched candelabrum specific for *Hanukkah*. Even though the word *hanukkiah* is the correct term for the candelabrum used on *Hanukkah*, Jews still generally refer to *hanukkiahs* as *menorahs*.

9

Display Having Selectable Simulated Illuminating Means

U.S. Patent Number: 5,881,482

Inventor: David Goldman

Date Issued: March 16, 1999

Problem: *Hanukkah* cards often have a depiction of a *menorah* with all nine candles lit. But is there a way to make a *Hanukkah* card that can vary the number of lit candles shown to represent which day of *Hanukkah* it is?

How the Problem is Solved: This invention is for a *Hanukkah* card that has a rotatable wheel with holes that allow back light to pass through to the front of the card. When you rotate the wheel to correspond to the day of *Hanukkah*, the correct number of candles appear to be lit on the front of the card that shows the *menorah*.

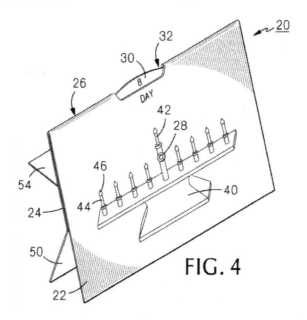

FIG. 4

Illuminated Window Display Ornament

U.S. Patent Number: 5,315,492

Inventor: Donald Davenport

Date Issued: May 24, 1994

Problem: Hanging lit objects, such as *menorahs*, on a window is difficult because of the required attachment means and electrical connections required. It would be unaesthetic and dangerous to have wires hanging from a *menorah* attached to a window. Is there a better way?

How the Problem is Solved: In this invention, the inventor discusses a few holiday ornaments, including a *menorah*, where the electric *menorah* is integrated with suction cups to attach it to a window. The *menorah* also has a battery holder so that LED lights on the candles can glow without the use of real candles or the need of an outlet.

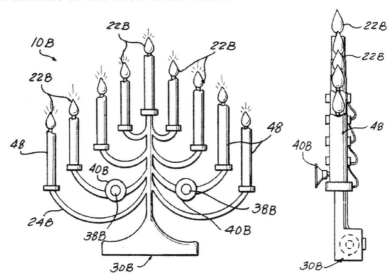

Collapsible Lighting Fixture

U.S. Patent Application Number: 14/054,750
(Patent Pending)

Inventor: Mitchell Bogart

Date Filed: October 15, 2013

Problem: Many Jewish organizations like to use a large *menorah* during *Hanukkah*. Some even like their *menorahs* to be transportable. But large *menorahs* are difficult to transport because of the nine branches. Is there a way to make a large *menorah* easily transportable?

How the Problem is Solved: In this patent pending application, eight of the branches (arms) are removable from the center arm. The arms are connected to each other in a way other so that all the arms can collapse as shown in the illustrations below.

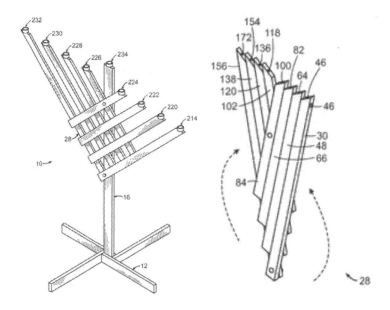

Illuminated Dreidel

U.S. Patent Number: 7,909,674

Inventor: Raphael Goozner

Date Issued: March 22, 2011

Problem: A *dreidel* is a four-sided spinning top with a Hebrew letter on each side. The letters are *nun*, *gimel*, *hay* and *shin* (or *peh*), and stand for the phrase, "A great miracle happened there/here."[9] The *dreidel* is used for a simple gambling game where players can either take or put money into a pot depending on what letter the *dreidel* lands on. Can you spice up this game a little bit with a special *dreidel*?

How the Problem is Solved: In this invention, the handle of the *dreidel* is not only used for spinning the *dreidel*, but by pressing the handle down, the *dreidel* lights up, and by pressing the handle down again, the *dreidel* light turns off.

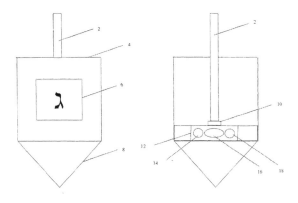

---

[9] Whether the fourth letter on a *dreidel* is a *shin* or a *peh* depends on whether the *dreidel* is meant for use inside or outside of Israel. The letter *peh* is the first letter of the word *poh*, meaning "here." The letter *shin* is the first letter of the word *sham*, meaning "there." Since the miracle of *Hanukkah* occurred in Israel, *dreidels* used inside and outside of Israel are different to reflect whether the miracle happened "here" or "there."

Active Hanukkah Candelabrum

U.S. Patent Number: 6,491,516

Inventors: Guy Tal and Ran Tal

Date Issued: December 10, 2002

Problem: You've already learned about *menorahs* and *dreidels*. Is there a way to combine the fun of both a *menorah* and a *dreidel* into a combined device for *Hanukkah* celebrations?

How the Problem is Solved: This invention is for a wireless connection between a *dreidel* and a *menorah*. As the *dreidel* spins, it transmits a signal to the *menorah*. When the *menorah* receives the transmitted signal from the *dreidel*, it lights up or plays music.

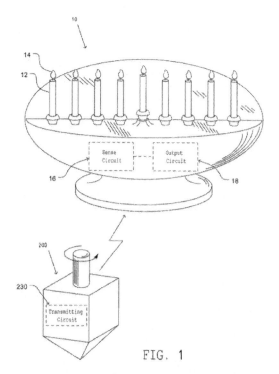

FIG. 1

Retractable Sukkah Awning

U.S. Patent Number: 6,024,153

Inventor: Tzvi Goldman

Date Issued: February 15, 2000

Problem: A *sukkah* is a temporary hut representative of the huts lived in when the Jews wandered in the desert after they escaped slavery in Egypt. Every year, Jews recreate the experience by living in, or at least eating in, a *sukkah* during the holiday of *Sukkot*. But if it rains you will get wet because the roof of the *sukkah* is just made from vegetative matter.

How the Problem is Solved: This invention is for a retractable awning used as a roof for the *sukkah*. The roof diverts water to the edge of the *sukkah*. This type of cover would not be used by observant Jews since the roof is required to be made from *schach* which is raw, unfinished vegetable matter (e.g. lumber, bamboo, evergreen branches, reeds, corn stalks, etc.). Furthermore, Jewish law says that one must be able to see stars through the roof. The retractable awning in this patent is not made of *schach* and you would not be able to see stars through it.

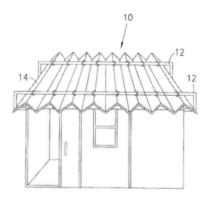

Temporary Building Structure

U.S. Patent Number: 4,584,801

Inventor: Edward Weinberger

Date Issued: April 29, 1986

Problem: The *sukkah* must be sturdy enough to permit usage for eating, entertaining, and provide a general living area, but also should be easy to assemble and take down without excessive cost, manpower, or time. How can this be accomplished?

How the Problem is Solved: This invention is for a *sukkah* kit. The base beams of the *sukkah* are stepped and overlap at each base corner. There are a combination of holes, notches, upright studs, and pins arranged in a specific way for quick assembly of the *sukkah*. Details of the kit can be seen in the actual patent.

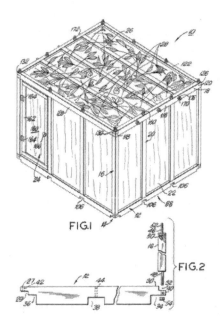

FIG.1

FIG.2

Modular Structures and Panels for Constructing Them

U.S. Patent Number: 7,677,006

Inventors: Stephen Rozenberg and James Zumpone

Date Issued: March 16, 2010

Problem: Modular *sukkah* structures come in pieces to be assembled by the user. Many *sukkahs* use small pieces and require a fair amount of manual dexterity. Can the *sukkah* structure and assembly of it be improved?

How the Problem is Solved: The inventors claim that their *sukkah* invention is ideal for people with low manual dexterity and does not have many small pieces. The *sukkah* comes with a panel having a male edge to fit within a channel of a female edge of another panel. The panels do not have to be lifted or rotated. The *sukkah* also uses a number slidable latches that can lock and release the male and female panels with each other.

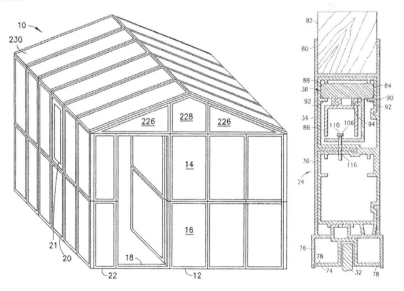

Noisemaker

U.S. Patent Number: 5,073,139

Inventor: Jacob Kassarich

Date Issued: December 17, 1991

Problem: During the holiday of *Purim*, Jews read the Book of Esther. The Book of Esther tells the story of Queen Esther and her uncle Mordechai who stopped a man named Haman from annihilating the Jews of Persia. During the reading of the Book of Esther, Haman's name is supposed to be drowned out in noise. The most common way to drown out Haman's name is through the use of a device called a *gragger*, which is a simple sprocket and bar that makes noise when rotated. Can this simple noisemaker be improved to make it more entertaining?

How the Problem is Solved: In this invention, the *gragger* lights up and blinks via the use of a centripetal force lever switch embedded in the housing. When the *gragger* spins, the switch completes an electrical circuit that causes lights in the *gragger* to turn on.

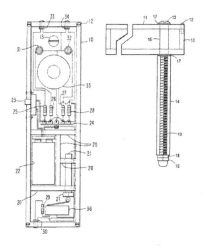

Cup Having Illusion of Emptying Content

U.S. Patent Number: 3,733,071

Inventor: Maxine Levin

Date Issued: May 15, 1973

Problem: During the holiday of *Pesach* (Passover) there is a tradition that the prophet Elijah visits every home and drinks some wine from a special goblet placed on the table for him. At a specific time during the *Pesach* meal the door is opened to welcome in Elijah. Everyone jokes that it looks like there's less wine after Elijah enters, but in reality, you can't see a difference in the wine level, if some wine has evaporated during the evening. Can you make it look like Elijah really drank his wine?

How the Problem is Solved: This is invention is for a "trick" wine goblet. There is a transparent upper section and an opaque hollow base. A valve between the upper and lower section can be opened so that the wine level drops as the wine goes from the upper transparent section to the opaque region. It therefore looks like Elijah drank his wine.

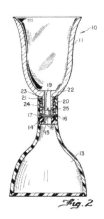

Fig. 2

Chapter 2
Sacred Text Patents

The *Torah*, also known as the "Five Books of Moses," is the most sacred text in Judaism. The *Torah* is also the first part of what Christians call "The Old Testament." It tells the story of the Jewish people from the creation of the universe through the death of Moses, Judaism's greatest prophet. The *Torah* is not only a history of the Jewish people, but is an instruction book for how to live a moral and spiritual life according to G-d's plan.

Although the *Torah* can be printed in the form of a regular book, in order for a *Torah* to be acceptable for use during a prayer service, it must be hand written on animal parchment by a highly trained *Torah* scribe called a *sofer*. The parchment is made into a scroll and is wound around cylindrical rollers at two ends. As you read through the text of the *Torah*, you rotate the rollers to advance through the *Torah* sections. When not in use, the *Torah* is wrapped in a beautifully decorated covering and stored in an ark.[10]

There are probably hundreds if not thousands of sacred Jewish texts, but all patents relating to sacred Jewish texts are either directed to the *Torah* or a *mezuzah*. Like the *Torah*, a *mezuzah* is also a handwritten scroll, but much smaller (a few inches). A *mezuzah* is mounted to the right side of the doorpost

---

[10] An ark is an ornamental storage cabinet for a *Torah*.

of a Jewish home, and also mounted on most rooms inside of a home. The reason why Jews place a *mezuzah* on the doorpost is because of a verse in Deuteronomy, which says, "And you shall write them on the doorposts of your house, and upon your gates." (Deuteronomy 6:9). The actual words written in the *mezuzah* include the most important words of Judaism, the *Shema*. The *Shema* is usually translated as "Hear O Israel, the Lord our G-d, the Lord is one" and encapsulates the essence of the Jewish statement of faith, that there is one G-d.

Torah Crown

U.S. Patent Application Number: 13/741,768
(Patent Pending)

Inventor: Yakov Merdinger

Date Filed: January 15, 2013

Problem: The *Torah* is not kept bare without a cover when it is stored in an ark. The *Torah* is generally wrapped in a beautiful cloth adorned with artwork, and the *Torah* scroll handles are adorned with decorative crowns. The crowns and cloth cover are removed during the *Torah* service so the *Torah* can be laid out on a podium and chanted. Usually the *Torah* crowns are placed on the scroll handles without any attachment mechanism, so they might fall off if you are not careful when carrying the *Torah*.

How the Problem is Solved: This invention is for a *Torah* crown having two latching mechanisms to hold the crown to a base that is placed over the top of the *Torah*, as shown in the figures below.

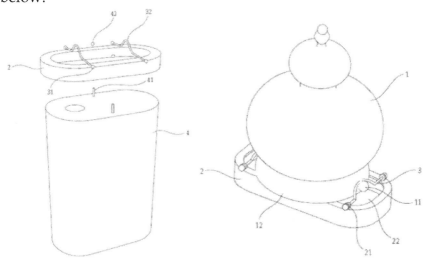

Apparatus and Method for Facilitating Scrolling of a Scrollable Document

U.S. Patent Number: 6,581,869

Inventor: Yehuda Arrane

Date Issued: June 24, 2003

Problem: Many Jewish religious texts are written on scrolls. The *Torah* is one such text and is written on parchment bound at two roller ends. When the *Torah* is read, it is usually placed on a podium, and as you progress through the chapters of the *Torah*, you rotate the roller ends to advance the parchment. This constant rolling can be cumbersome. Is there a better a way to make it easier to advance through text of the *Torah*?

How the Problem is Solved: In this invention there are a pair of tracks that hold the two rollers. For each roller there is a pair of sliders. This assembly enables the *Torah* to be easily moved along the track as well as easily wound and unwound on the roller ends.

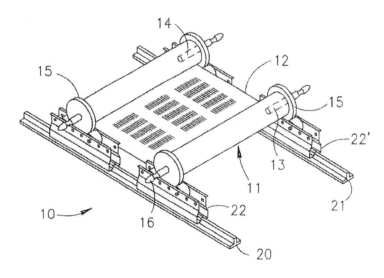

Color-Coded Melody Text and Method of Teaching

U.S. Patent Number: 6,639,139

Inventor: Richard Muller

Date Issued: October 28, 2003

Problem: During the *Torah* service, the words of the *Torah* are chanted, not just read. Each word of the *Torah* is chanted with a specific melody, but the words in the *Torah* used for a service do not have musical notes written alongside the text. However, to practice chanting the *Torah*, you can use a book that has the melody of each word right next to each word. Instead of Western style notes written next to each word, a symbol, called a *trope*, indicates each word's melody. There are around 20 *Torah tropes*, that is, each word of the Torah is chanted in one of about 20 melodies, each *trope* a few notes long. Some people may have trouble remembering which *trope* symbol applies to what melody, so is there a way to help the *Torah* reader learn the right melody without using *tropes*?

How the Problem is Solved: Here, instead of using *tropes* to learn *Torah* melodies, this method of teaching *Torah* chanting uses a color-coded system, where each color is associated with a *trope* melody. Shown below, instead of colors, the words are boxed in with different types of lines that represent colors. The different boxes represent the different melodies of the *Torah* words.

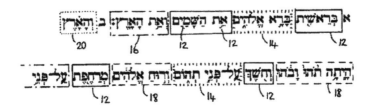

Reading Assistant for Torah Scrolls

U.S. Patent Number: 7,469,494

Inventors: Dov Katz et al.

Date Issued: December 30, 2008

Problem: As previously described, the words in a *Torah* scroll do not have *tropes* (musical symbol notations) written directly in the *Torah*. The words in a *Torah* scroll also do not have any vowels. If you have a memory lapse during a *Torah* reading for how to chant or pronounce the words, there are no visual clues to help you through it. Is there a failsafe way to remember the pronunciation and melody of the *Torah* portion during a *Torah* service?

How the Problem is Solved: In this invention, a light box and notation sheet having vowels and *tropes* are placed under the *Torah* parchment so that you can see the vowels and *tropes* projected through the *Torah* as you chant the *Torah* portion for that day.

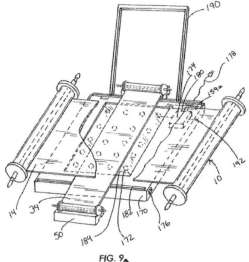

FIG. 9a

Method for Projecting Signs Printed on Matter and Means for the Same

U.S. Patent Number: 7,236,144

Inventor: Amichai Ben Ari

Date Issued: June 26, 2007

Problem: As discussed previously, the *Torah* used in a service does not have any vowels or *tropes*. We've seen a couple ways for the *Torah* reader to remember the correct pronunciations and melodies associated with the *Torah's* words, but are there other ways to accomplish the same thing?

How the Problem is Solved: This invention is for a method of making a transparent sheet to be aligned with the *Torah*. The transparent sheet has vowels, *tropes*, and punctuation, which can be placed over the *Torah* scroll to help the *Torah* reader know how to pronounce and chant the *Torah*. The sheet can be shifted as you progress through different *Torah* portions.

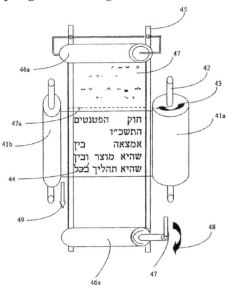

Writing Utensil

U.S. Patent Number: 8,915,665

Inventor: Eliahou Gozlan

Date Issued: December 23, 2014

Problem: Sacred texts, such as the *Torah*, must be written by a highly trained scribe using a special kind of thick black ink. The viscosity of the ink requires pressing the tip of a pen, called a nib, against the parchment. However, pressing the nib against the rough *Torah* parchment can wear down the soft quill that makes up the nib. Is there a way to improve the nib of a pen used for writing *Torahs*?

How the Problem is Solved: This invention is for an improved nib that is made of ceramic and has a tube with a slanted distal opening. The nib also has a groove extending from the tip along the interior wall of the nib. There is also a slit that extends from the tip along a part of the nib. The inventor contends that this is an improvement over other nibs used for *Torah* writing.

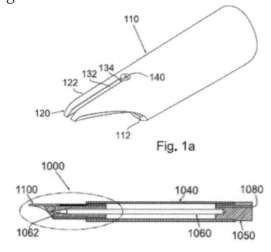

Fig. 1a

Mezuzah Case

U.S. Patent Number: 8,269,621

Inventor: Tomer Shapira and Eli Levi

Date Issued: September 18, 2012

Problem: On the doorpost of every Jewish home is an object called a *mezuzah*. A *mezuzah* is a parchment scroll with two paragraphs from the book of Deuteronomy. When a Jew enters a home or room with a *mezuzah*, it is customary to touch the *mezuzah* case and then kiss the hand that touched the case. But what if you forget that you are entering a home with a *mezuzah*?

How the Problem is Solved: In this invention, the inventor combines a *mezuzah* and *mezuzah* case with a battery operated motion detector so that when there is movement near the *mezuzah*, a light or sound emits from the case to draw attention to the *mezuzah*, so you remember to kiss it.

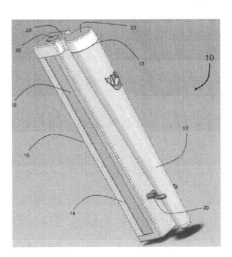 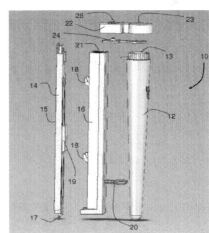

Door Post-Attachable
Housing for a Parchment

U.S. Patent Number: 6,702,107

Inventor: Zeev Raz

Date Issued: March 9, 2004

Problem: As previously described, a *mezuzah* is a parchment scroll, but it is not very practical to place a piece of parchment directly on the doorpost because the parchment would be exposed to the elements. To protect the parchment, *mezuzahs* are enclosed within a *mezuzah* case that is secured to the doorpost. The case with the *mezuzah* is then secured to the doorpost. In most *mezuzah* casings, it is impossible to access the *mezuzah* parchment once the case is mounted on a doorpost, unless you pry it off.[11] Can a *mezuzah* and its case have features that overcome this problem?

How the Problem is Solved: In this invention, the *mezuzah* case has a base that is secured to the doorpost. The base has a compartment to hold the scroll and a removable cover to fit over the base that engages with the base, as shown below.

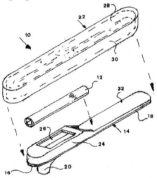

---

[11] You occasionally remove the *mezuzah* scroll from the casing every few years to check whether the *mezuzah* parchment is still decent shape.

Mezuzah

U.S. Patent Number: 6,006,900

Inventor: Mark Hasten

Date Issued: December 28, 1999

Problem: As previously described, a *mezuzah* should be placed on the doorpost of the entryway of a home and on the doorposts for most rooms in the house. According to tradition, the *mezuzah* should be checked at least twice every seven years to make sure that there are no problems with the text, such as deteriorated letters. However, once the *mezuzah* is secured to the doorpost, it can be difficult to remove the scroll to check it. Is there an easier way to access the *mezuzah* after it has been secured to the doorpost, rather than prying it off?

How the Problem is Solved: In this invention, the *mezuzah* housing has a base member that is permanently attached to the doorpost and a housing member with a bore to place the scroll. The housing member engages by sliding with the base member and can be secured with a latch to selectively prevent the housing member from disengaging with the base member.

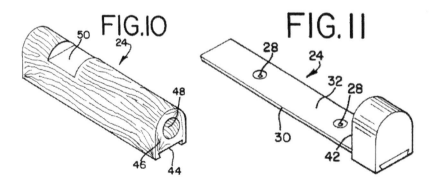

Yad Including Mezuzah Casement

U.S. Patent Number: 8,485,352

Inventor: Daniel Hawtof

Date Issued: July 16, 2013

Problem: The physical words written on the parchment of the *Torah* scroll are considered sacred. Therefore it is customary that bare fingers not touch the words in the *Torah*. Instead of using your fingers to keep track of your position while reading the *Torah*, a decorative pointer (called a *yad*) in the shape of a hand, is used to help you keep track of your position. A *mezuzah*, as previously described, comprises two paragraphs of Hebrew text secured to the doorpost of your home. Can we combine the *yad* and *mezuzah* into a single device?

How the Problem is Solved: This invention includes a *yad* with a compartment for a *mezuzah* scroll. The *yad* and scroll are configured in a way so that they can be inserted into a backing plate that is already attached to the doorpost for *mezuzah* placement. The *yad* can be removed when you want to read the *Torah* (but then you would not have *mezuzah* on your doorpost).

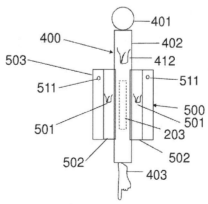

Chapter 3
Shabbat Patents

Acchording to the book of Genesis, G-d created the world in six days, "and on the seventh day, He rested from all His work." (Genesis 2:2). *Shabbat* (the Hebrew word for Sabbath) literally means "rest" or "cessation." Just as G-d rested on the seventh day, *Shabbat*, so should the Jews. By resting on *Shabbat* and ceasing from work, Jews attempt to emulate the divine and take a step back from the material world one day per week. This weekly time of rest is said to be the closest thing in this world to what we will have in *ha-olam ha-ba* (the world to come). *Shabbat* begins Friday evening as the sun sets, and lasts until after sunset on Saturday night.

There are probably more laws regarding *Shabbat* observance than any other aspect of Jewish life. While Jewish law (*halacha*) prohibits work (*melacha*) on *Shabbat*, the English translation of the Hebrew word *melacha* to "work" is not very accurate. Not everything you might consider "work" in today's society is prohibited on *Shabbat* and there are many actions that are prohibited on *Shabbat* that you might not consider work. Generally, the work that is prohibited on *Shabbat* relates to activities involving creation or destruction.

What Activities are Prohibited on Shabbat?

Although the *Torah* does not specifically list all the activities that are prohibited on *Shabbat*, the *Torah* juxtaposes the commandment to cease work on *Shabbat* with its instructions on how to build the *miskhan*.[12] The rabbis of the *Talmud* (a collection of compiled laws and commentary on the *Torah*) deduced 39 prohibited activities on *Shabbat* related to building the *mishkan*, which are divided into six groups of activities listed below:

Field Work: (1) sowing, (2) plowing, (3), reaping, (4) binding sheaves, (5) threshing, (6) winnowing, (7) selecting, (8) grinding, (9) sifting, (10) kneading, and (11) baking;

Making Material Curtains: (12) shearing wool, (13) cleaning, (14) combing, (15) dyeing, (16) spinning, (17) stretching threads, (18) making loops, (19) weaving threads, (20) separating threads, (21) tying a knot, (22) untying a knot, (23) sewing, and (24) tearing;

Making Leather Curtains: (25) trapping, (26) slaughtering, (27) skinning, (28) tanning, (29) smoothing, (30) ruling lines, and (31) cutting;

Making Beams of the Mishkan: (32) writing and (33) erasing;

The Putting up and Taking Down of the Mishkan: (34) building, (35) breaking down; and,

---

[12] The *mishkan* was the portable version of the Holy Temple that the Jews carried with them while wandering through desert after leaving slavery in Egypt.

The Miskhan's Final Touches: (36) extinguishing a fire, (37) kindling a fire, (38) striking the final hammer blow, and (39) carrying.

These 39 prohibited activities have subcategories that are also prohibited.

Electricity on *Shabbat*

You might be familiar with the fact that observant Jews do not use electricity on *Shabbat*. Yet nowhere in the list of prohibited activities is there a ban on the use of electricity because human use of electricity did not exist during the time that the *Talmud* was codified. However, Jewish law is not stuck in the past. Jewish law is constantly being interpreted to work in the modern world.

So why is the use of electricity on *Shabbat* prohibited? There is a well-known adage, "Ask two Jews a question, get three opinions." This adage reflects the wide disagreement on certain *halachic* issues for what is allowed and what is prohibited according to Jewish law, or even the reasons for the prohibitions. In this regard, various rationales have been set forth for why one should not turn on or off electrical devices during *Shabbat*. Some authorities have compared completing an electrical circuit to igniting a fire (a prohibited activity). Other authorities have asserted that turning on a switch completes an electrical circuit, which is akin to creating a building, and turning off an electrical switch is akin to destroying a building, both prohibited activities. Still other authorities have argued that by turning on an electrical switch, a power plant would burn more fuel, and since igniting a fire (using the fuel) is prohibited, so should turning on an electric device.

Although it is generally agreed that Jews may not switch on and off electrical devices during *Shabbat*, there is generally no prohibition against the continued use of an electrical device that is already on before *Shabbat* begins. For example, an observant Jew does not have to sit in a dark house or unplug the refrigerator before *Shabbat* begins. In addition to the continued enjoyment of devices that are already on before *Shabbat* begins, observant Jews often use pre-set timing devices to turn lights on and off during *Shabbat* so that, for example, house lights can be set to stay on from 6pm to 11pm, but turn off at 11pm. Another way to work around the prohibition of completing electrical circuits on *Shabbat* is through the principle of *grama*. *Grama* does not have an adequate English translation, but can generally be described as "indirect causation." If you perform an action that only indirectly causes an electrical circuit to complete, then this action may be permitted according to some authorities. However, what constitutes *grama* and what does not constitute *grama* is hotly debated even amongst very observant Jews.

The following 25 patents are for inventions that make doing things on *Shabbat* easier. These patents relate to flipping switches in a manner that might be allowed during *Shabbat*, cooking, using hot water, using elevators, using a telephone, dimming lights, and amplifying sound. There are a variety of opinions regarding what actions constitute a prohibited activity on *Shabbat*, and the author expresses no opinion regarding whether the use of these devices is permitted on *Shabbat* or not. While some authorities may permit the use of these inventions, others would not. If you are *shomer shabbos* (Sabbath observant), consult your rabbi before using any of these devices.

Arrangement for Preventing Operation of an Electric Switch

U.S. Patent Number: 4,506,120

Inventor: Jonas Fleischman

Date Issued: March 19, 1985

Problem: Although there are complicated ways to prevent using electricity on *Shabbat*, is there an ultra low-tech and cheap way to prevent you from inadvertently flipping a switch?

How the Problem is Solved: This invention is for a snap-on switch blocker that connects around the screws that secure the switch wall plate to the wall. It is impossible to inadvertently flip a switch on or off when this device covers the switch. The device can easily be snapped on before *Shabbat* and snapped off after *Shabbat* ends.

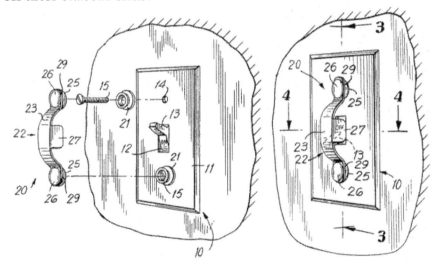

Method and Apparatus for a Geographically Determined Jewish Religious Clock and Electrical Device Combination with Holiday and Preference Modes

U.S. Patent Number: 9,024,545

Inventors: Yonason Bloch et al.

Date Issued: May 5, 2015

Problem: As previously discussed, one way to prevent completing electrical circuits is to physically cover the switch. If you don't want to cover up all your switches before *Shabbat* starts, is there a way to prevent an electrical circuit completion even if you accidentally flip a switch?

How the Problem is Solved: In this invention, a regular wall switch is replaced with a switch having functions that allow it to act as a normal switch, but has a *Shabbat*/holiday mode that electrically de-activates the switch at preprogrammed times, such as during the hours of *Shabbat*.

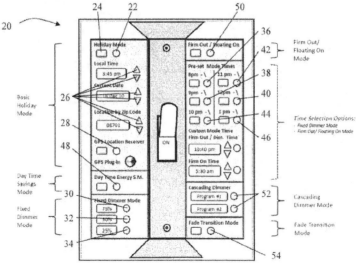

Sabbath Switch for Appliance

U.S. Patent Number: 6,974,925

Inventor: Jonathan Whitman

Date Issued: December 13, 2005

Problem: What should you do if you get hungry and want to open the refrigerator on *Shabbat*? There are actually a couple of *halachic* issues that arise when opening a refrigerator door on *Shabbat*. One is that most refrigerators have a light switch that turns on a light when the door opens. Some Jews solve this problem by using a very low tech solution of placing a piece of tape over the switch on *Shabbat*, but that method may not be as reliable as this patented device since the piece of tape can fall off.

How the Problem is Solved: This invention is for a switch cover that has an adhesive backing and slidable member that covers the light switch of the refrigerator so that when you open the refrigerator, the light switch remains in its down (off) position. Before *Shabbat* begins, you merely slide the slidable member down over the switch, as shown in the figures below. When *Shabbat* is over, you can slide the slidable member back up into its backing.

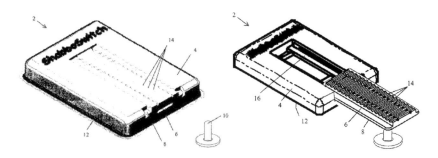

Home Automation System

U.S. Patent Number: 6,473,661

Inventor: Peter Wollner

Date Issued: March 15, 2002

Problem: Although some observant Jews leave the lights on for the entirety of *Shabbat*, others prefer systems where lights go on and off at particular times. Simple mechanical timers are useful but usually only control a single lamp or appliance. Whole home automated electrical control systems exist but are based on the Gregorian calendar and secular times, not the Jewish calendar and Jewish times. Secular times are not relevant for the observant Jew, since *Shabbat* and holiday times vary because the sun sets at different times throughout the year.

How the Problem is Solved: This invention for a home automation system includes a programmed computer with the Jewish calendar and times. The programming accounts for different daylight lengths throughout the year, and holiday time requirements.

Switching Device and Method

U.S. Patent Number: 7,872,576

Inventor: Andreh Kalatizadeh

Date Issued: January 18, 2011

Problem: Although Jews are prohibited from completing electrical circuits, some authorities are lenient when it comes to completing circuits if there are "mitigating factors." Can you take advantage of "mitigating factors" as part of a switch to make its use allowable on *Shabbat*?

How the Problem is Solved: This invention uses a number of "mitigating factors" that might allow some observant Jews to use an electrical switch on *Shabbat*. One "mitigating factor" is whether there is a delay from an initial action to an ultimate result. For example, a mitigating factor might be a delay from flipping a switch to when the electrical circuit is actually completed. This device uses a random number generator to delay a transmission from a transmitter to a receiver. The details are complex, but the use of a random number generator with a switch to delay transmission of a signal adds an element of unpredictability to the direct causal link of flipping the switch to the electrical connection. Some authorities allow this type of switch on *Shabbat*, while others do not.

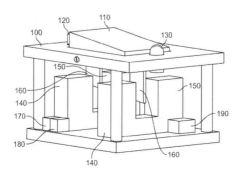

41

Locking Mechanism
With Sabbath Control Unit

U.S. Patent Number: 8,466,786

Inventor: Asher Haviv

Date Issued: June 18, 2013

Problem: An observant Jew is prohibited from setting a home alarm system on *Shabbat* because pushing buttons to set the alarm would complete electrical circuits. Can a Jew set an alarm when leaving the house during *Shabbat*?

How the Problem is Solved: In this invention, there is a light beam inside of a locking mechanism (such as deadbolt lock). The beam hits a sensor connected to an alarm unit. When you turn the lock, the light beam is blocked, which the sensor detects, and then turns the alarm on. While some authorities consider that blocking a light beam for the purpose of triggering a circuit to later turn on a device is prohibited, others say that this type of mechanism is allowable.

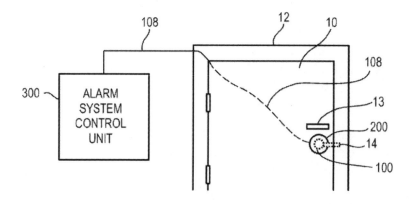

Timer for Operating Electric Appliance at Saturday and Holyday According to Jewish Religious Law

U.S. Patent Number: 8,067,706

Inventor: Ezra Tukachinsky

Date Issued: November 29, 2011

Problem: Timers are often set before *Shabbat* so that electrical appliances can be used during *Shabbat*. However, timers can be inflexible. Let's say that you are not sure what time you want to the lights to go on and off during the *Shabbat*, but you know that you definitely do want the option of delaying the lights either turning on or off during *Shabbat*.

How the Problem is Solved: This invention uses a first timing device that activates and deactivates an appliance from time to time, and a second timing device delays the appliance deactivating from the first timing device. During *Shabbat* you can adjust the second timing device (the delay device) to the amount of time the appliance should be on. Since delaying circuit completion using non-electric means does not complete a circuit directly, some authorities permit using this type of delay mechanism on *Shabbat*.

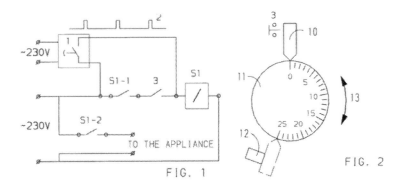

FIG. 1

FIG. 2

Switching Device

U.S. Patent Number: 4,031,435

Inventors: Dov Zioni and Levi Halperin

Date Issued: June 21, 1977

Problem: As described previously, any type of switch used on *Shabbat* must have specific characteristics for it to even have a chance of having a permitted use on *Shabbat*. One characteristic of a possibly permitted switch for an electrical circuit is that the final activation or termination of the system should not be the direct result of an initial activation, such as the initial activation of a person pressing a pushbutton. Can this principle be used to operate a switch during *Shabbat*?

How the Problem is Solved: This is a technically complex invention that cannot be adequately explained without detailed knowledge of electronics. Briefly though, the inductor of a circuit is adapted to be periodically pulse energized. An armature of the device is movably mounted to assume a first and second position relative to the inductor, thereby causing a distinct variation of current flow in the inductor when energized by the periodically applied pulse. Since the final activation of the electric circuit is not directly caused by the initial activation of pressing a button, some authorities permit its use on *Shabbat*.

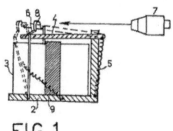

FIG.1

Refrigerator Control Including a Hidden Features Menu

U.S. Patent Number: 7,827,811

Inventors: J. Ferragut Nelson and Robert Wetekamp

Date Issued: November 9, 2010

Problem: Let's say that you want a refrigerator that has a "*Shabbat* mode,"[13] but for some reason you don't want others to know that you have a special refrigerator, or you're a company that wants to cater to observant Jews, but don't want non-Jews to be turned off to purchasing a "strange" *Shabbat* refrigerator. Is there a way to cater to everyone?

How the Problem is Solved: This refrigerator has a hidden feature menu. One of the hidden features is a "*Shabbat* mode." Observant Jews would know which refrigerators have *Shabbat* modes through word of mouth or selective advertising, but it is likely that the general public would have no idea that their refrigerator has a "*Shabbat* mode." Would you know?

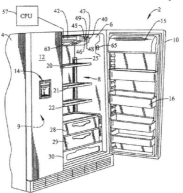

---

[13] A "*Shabbat* mode" is a setting where no lights turn on when the door is opened, and the cooling mechanism is not directly linked to temperature changes caused by a person opening the refrigerator door.

Control System for Cooking Appliance During Jewish Holidays and Sabbath

U.S. Patent Number: 8,669,501

Inventor: Myron Frommer

Date Issued: March 11, 2014

Problem: During *Shabbat* it is prohibited to start or extinguish fires, or to complete or disrupt electrical circuits. How can you cook (or warm items) on *Shabbat* if you can't start a fire? Or are you prohibited from cooking altogether?

How the Problem is Solved: Even though you cannot start fires, or complete electrical circuits during *Shabbat*, you are allowed to set programs to start fires or complete circuits if the programming was done before *Shabbat* began.[14] This invention is for a *Shabbat* time control system connected to an oven. You can set a time for an oven/burner to turn on or off, as well as set an oven temperature before *Shabbat* begins.

FIG. 1

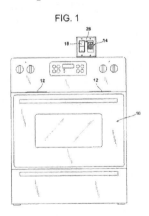

---

[14] Even though fires may be started by timers, many authorities still say that you should not cook food on *Shabbat*, but you can keep it warm.

Electronic Appliance and a Sabbath Mode

U.S. Patent Number: 5,808,278

Inventors: Chang Hwan Moon et al.

Date Issued: September 15, 1998

Problem: Observant Jews often will turn their ovens on before *Shabbat* begins and keep it on for the entirety of *Shabbat*. But if you don't want to leave your oven on all day, is there another way to use your oven to cook (or at least warm) food? Some ovens also have lights that turn on when you door is opened, or a digital display might change when you open the door. If these things occur when you open the oven door, then opening the oven door would be prohibited on *Shabbat*.

How the Problem is Solved: This invention is for a control system that keeps the light either on or off regardless of when the door is open, disables audio alarms on the oven, and delays activating heating unit when the temperature drops due to the oven door being open.

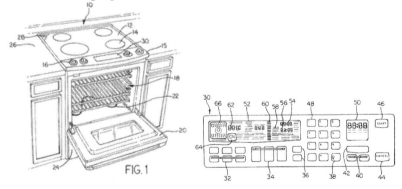

FIG. 1

Method and Apparatus for Sabbath Compliance Cooking Apparatus

U.S. Patent Number: 6,066,837

Inventor: DeWayne McCormick and Dindo Uy

Date Issued: May 23, 2000

Problem: The reason for the necessity of *Shabbat* mode ovens has been described previously. But is there more than one way to design a *Shabbat* mode to overcome the various problems with using normal ovens on *Shabbat*?

How the Problem is Solved: In this invention, once the oven is placed in *Shabbat* mode, the lights remain in the status that it was in before *Shabbat*. Other programs on the oven can be set or disabled until *Shabbat* is over. To understand the detailed differences between the different Shabbat ovens, you will have to read the entirety of the patents.

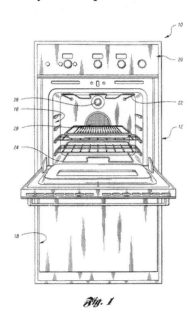

Fig. 1

Method and Apparatus for Shabbos/Yom Tov Appliance Control

U.S. Patent Number: 6,703,591

Inventor: Wolfgang Daum et al.

Date Issued: March 9, 2004

Problem: As previously described, many appliances have functions that are not permitted for use on *Shabbat* because these functions involve completing an electrical circuit. What functions can be integrated so that the appliance is *Shabbat* compatible?

How the Problem is Solved: This invention describes a few *Shabbat* compatible oven devices. One is for a control system that has a random time delay from a user pressing a button to the result being shown on the display. Since there is a delay from when the button is pressed to when it completes a circuit, some authorities allow using this device on *Shabbat*. Other functions on the display interface are disabled completely on *Shabbat*.

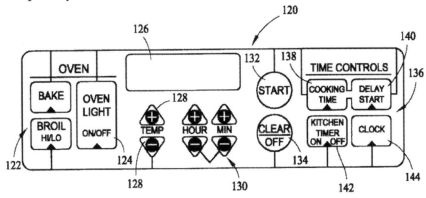

Water Dispenser With Sabbath Function

U.S. Patent Number: 7,672,576

Inventor: Ilan Grossbach

Date Issued: March 2, 2010

Problem: Just as there is a prohibition of turning on or off electrical devices on *Shabbat*, there is also a prohibition of heating water during *Shabbat* because heating water involves cooking, starting a fire, or completing an electrical circuit. Many homes have a water dispenser (such as Sparkletts) for dispensing water. These types of dispensers have a large jug of water on top of a smaller water holding reservoir that can be heated. The heated reservoir is connected to a hot water spigot. When you dispense hot water, new cold water falls into the reservoir, and the heating element turns on to heat the new cold water in the reservoir. Therefore, the act of dispensing hot water causes a heating element to turn on, which would be prohibited on *Shabbat*.

How the Problem is Solved: This invention is for a water dispenser that has a *Shabbat* mode. In this mode, the heating element is constantly on to keep the water at a particular temperature, and a valve prevents the jug from releasing new water into the vessel so that no new water is heated on *Shabbat*.

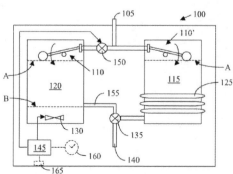

Sabbath Urn Having Associated Second Vessel and Accessories Thereof

European Patent Number: 1,618,818

Inventor: Avraham Soryas

Date Issued: January 25, 2006

Problem: It is generally prohibited on *Shabbat* to heat foods using liquids that are above around 104 degrees. The *halachic* reasonings for the various and specific cooking laws on *Shabbat* are well beyond the scope this book. Nevertheless, these laws generally prohibit the normal preparation of hot tea or coffee on *Shabbat* because the hot water used to make tea and coffee is above 104 degrees and "cooks" the coffee and tea leaves.

How the Problem is Solved: The prohibition of cooking foods with water above 104 degrees applies only to water that comes from the receptacle used to heat the water to 104 degrees. If an intermediate vessel is used to transfer the hot water to a separate vessel, then the water may be used, even if still above 104 degrees. This invention is for a unit that has two receptacles, 1) a heating unit urn, and 2) an auxiliary vessel that is not heated. When the heating unit urn liquid goes into the auxiliary vessel, you can use the hot water from the auxiliary vessel to make tea, coffee or other foods (even if above 104 degrees).

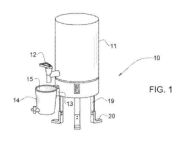

FIG. 1

Hot Liquid Dispenser

U.S. Patent Number: 7,974,527

Inventor: Eitan Adler

Date Issued: July 5, 2011

Problem: The invention by Soryas on the previous page is one way to design a system where hot water can be used to make coffee or tea without violating the laws of *Shabbat*. But is there way to design a hot water dispenser where the dispenser doesn't have the appearance of two separate pieces, and looks like a regular single unit water dispenser?

How the Problem is Solved: In this invention, there is a first chamber that has a heating element for heating water. The first chamber is connected to a second chamber fully enclosed in the interior space of the housing of the unit, but thermally insulated from the heating chamber. A conduit allows only one-way flow of liquid from the first chamber to the second chamber. This invention therefore allows you to have a normal looking hot water dispenser that is usable on *Shabbat*.

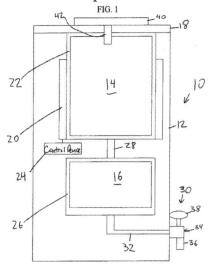

Sabbath Elevator

European Patent Number: 2,753,564

Inventor: Arie Yakuel and Hilel Yakovson

Date Issued: July 16, 2014

Problem: On *Shabbat* it is prohibited to directly actuate electrical equipment. Sabbath elevators have been designed to go to every floor with or without anyone pressing a button, which enables observant Jews to use them on *Shabbat*. However, even these elevators may pose a problem because elevators adjust the motor power based on the weight (load) in the elevator. So when you enter a normal elevator (or even some Sabbath elevators), the elevator measures your weight to determine the appropriate amount of power to use. Thus you are directly causing electrical connections to occur for measuring weight, and you are causing an increase in additional current to power the motor, which may be prohibited.

How the Problem is Solved: In this invention, the drive system uses stored energy in a non-electric energy accumulator, such as hydraulic, pneumatic, or gravitational potential energy. The energy accumulator is connected to a displacement mechanism that drives the motion of the elevator.

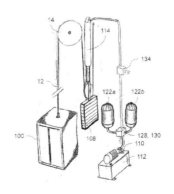

Load Cancelling Device for Conveyance Systems

U.S. Patent Number: 4,071,116

Inventors: Levi Halperin et al.

Date Issued: January 31, 1978

Problem: The purpose of *Shabbat* elevators has been previously been described, and typical elevators cannot be used on *Shabbat* because you complete an electrical circuit when selecting what floor to go to. Sometimes just the weight of a person may cause the electric motor to draw additional current, which would be prohibited on *Shabbat*. Is there any type of situation where an observant Jew can use an elevator on *Shabbat*?

How the Problem is Solved: The details of this invention are complex but involve a load-cancelling system that is adapted to cancel the effect of a load weight on the requirements from the power source so that no *Shabbat* laws are broken when you enter an elevator.

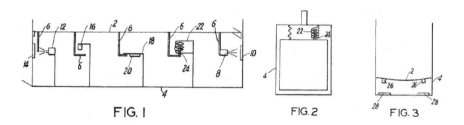

FIG. 1   FIG. 2   FIG. 3

System and Method for Pre-Programmable Elevator Operation

Patent Number: 8,499,895

Inventor: Zvi Zweig

Date Issued: August 6, 2013

Problem: *Shabbat* elevators usually stop at every single floor, but what if you live on the 8th floor and don't want to stop at every floor during *Shabbat*? Is there a way to design a *Shabbat* elevator that will accommodate stopping at only your particular floor without pressing any elevator buttons?

How the Problem is Solved: In this invention, the *Shabbat* elevator has a programmable unit where, before *Shabbat* begins, you can program which floors the elevator should go to at specified times. For example, the elevator can be set to go back and forth directly between the 8th floor and the ground floor between 7:30am and 8:30am. After that time period, the elevator may revert back to its normal mode.

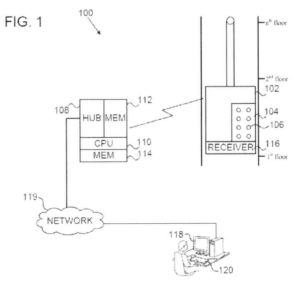

FIG. 1

Indirectly Activated Telephone System

U.S. Patent Number: 4,375,583

Inventors: Yitzhak Halperin and Dov Zioni

Date Issued: March 1, 1983

Problem: In old rotary phones, when you place your finger in the number hole, rotate the dial, and withdraw your finger, the dial rotates back to its initial position. As the dial rotates back to its original position, the dial sends a series of electrical pulses corresponding to the number dialed. However, this direct actuation of electrical impulses on a phone would not be allowed on *Shabbat*. Is there a way to use a rotary phone on *Shabbat*?

How the Problem is Solved: In this invention, when you rotate the dial, instead of reverting back to its default dial position, the dial is maintained in the rotated position for a pre-set amount of time, thereby separating the dialing action from the later electrical impulses.[15]

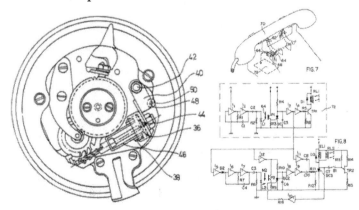

---

[15] All kinds of other electrical circuits are made when using a phone, so even if this one aspect may skirt some laws of *Shabbat*, a phone like this likely would violate other prohibitions on *Shabbat*.

Free-Standing (Self-Supporting) Lamp Shade

U.S. Patent Number: 4,809,145

Inventor: Martin Bennett

Date Issued: February 28, 1989

Problem: An observant Jew often wants to control the amount of light on *Shabbat* but cannot turn on or off switches, or even use dimmers. Is there a way to effectively dim a light on *Shabbat*?

How the Problem is Solved: This invention is for a lamp shade that is opaque to translucent. The shade covers the light but does not directly touch any part of the lamp or any associated electrical parts. There is a separate means for heat escape (such as ventilation holes) and support means, such as grooves on the shade base to hold the shade in place. An observant Jew can use this lamp shade to effectively dim or turn on and off a light or dim a light without changing any electrical circuits.

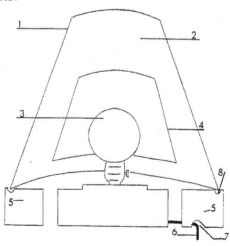

Fluid Sound Amplification System

U.S. Patent Number: 5,540,248

Inventors: Tadeusz Drzewiecki and R. Michael Phillippi

Date Issued: July 30, 1996

Problem: Sound amplifications systems such as microphones and speakers usually use electricity to amplify sound. However, since the use of electricity on *Shabbat* is prohibited, is there a way to amplify sound without electricity that would be permitted on *Shabbat*?

How the Problem is Solved: The details of this invention involve complicated fluid dynamics. This patent claims several different methods of amplifying a sound using principles of fluid dynamics and no electricity. One method couples two laminar proportional fluidic amplifiers (LPAs) and involves the steps of radiating an acoustic output signal through an unconfined air space and then receiving the output signal at a second LPA without directly coupling of the LPAs.

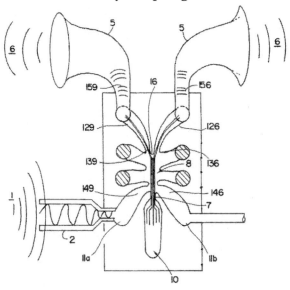

Synagogue Donation Recording Device

U.S. Patent Number: 2,514,451

Inventor: Hyman Krissoff

Date Issued: May 25, 1946

Problem: During *Shabbat*, Jews are prohibited from handling money. Unlike a church, where the church is supported by passing around a plate during services, Jews cannot give money at the time that they are most likely to be at the synagogue. Instead of passing around a plate, synagogues are usually supported by membership dues, but is there a way to "give money" on *Shabbat* without actually handling any money?

How the Problem is Solved: Instead of giving money directly, you pledge a specific amount, not by actually giving money, but by using a card that has slots and tabs for amounts of money that the member pledges to give at a later time. You can also pledge where you want your money to go, such as to the rabbi, or for the sick. These cards can be handled on *Shabbat*.

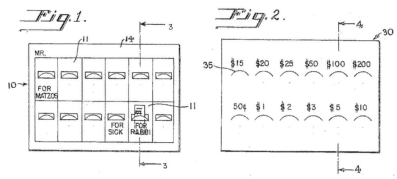

Candle Holder

U.S. Patent Number: 2,213,203

Inventor: Emil Buchman

Date Issued: September 30, 1940

Problem: On Friday night, before *Shabbat* begins, Jews light *Shabbat* candles to usher in the Sabbath. You are not allowed extinguish *Shabbat* candles during *Shabbat*, but since *Shabbat* candles can last hours, it might not be safe to keep the candles lit, especially if you plan to go to sleep before the candles extinguish themselves. How can you make sure that the *Shabbat* candles extinguish themselves in a reasonable amount of time?

How the Problem is Solved: This invention is for a spring-loaded device that fits around *Shabbat* candles. When the device is placed around the full circumference of the *Shabbat* candle, it is in an open position, but as the candle burns below the device tip, the top of the device closes due to the force of the spring, thereby extinguishing the flame, as shown below in the illustrations.

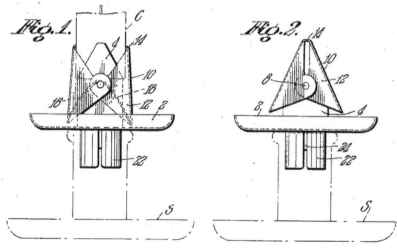

Picture Frame Tray System

U.S. Patent Number: 8,800,188

Inventor: Aaron Fishelis

Date Issued: August 12, 2014

Problem: To start *Shabbat*, it is traditional for the women of the household to light *Shabbat* candles. The lighting of the *Shabbat* candles signifies the end of the normal workweek and the beginning of the Sabbath, where no additional fires can be lit. Most households place the *Shabbat* candles on their dining room table, but what if you have a small table that cannot fit plates, utensils, food bowls, and *Shabbat* candles? Where should you place the candles?

How the Problem is Solved: This invention is for a picture frame that converts from a normal picture hung on a wall to a *Shabbat* candle holding tray. The frame is connected to the wall by a hinge mechanism that allows the picture to rotate down 90 degrees. The back of the picture is made of a fire resistant glass mirror that can support *Shabbat* candles.

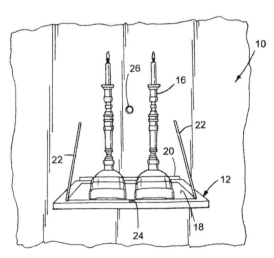

Chapter 4
Kashrut Patents

Kashrut is the body of Jewish law relating to food preparation and consumption. Foods that are in line with the laws of *kashrut* are said to be *kosher*, which means "fit," and those who follow the laws of *kashrut* are said to "keep kosher." The opposite of *kosher* is *treif*.

What is the reason for the laws of *kashrut*? The *Torah*, which is the primary source of all Jewish law, does not state the reason for the most of the laws of *kashrut*. Although there are an abundance of theories, for the observant Jew, one does not keep *kosher* because a particular theory has a rational explanation; rather, one keeps *kosher* to follow the laws set forth by G-d to lead a spiritually fulfilling life.

For non-Orthodox Jews that keep kosher, the reasons for keeping *kosher* vary. Some believe that the laws of *kashrut* are for health reasons and minimize animal cruelty.[16] Others believe that by keeping *kosher*, a Jew is constantly reminded throughout the day, every day, at every meal, of one's own

---

[16] While the health theory of *kashrut* may make sense in a few limited situations, such as the prohibition of pork to prevent illness caused by poor pork preparation, it is difficult to apply the health theory to the totality of the laws of *kashrut*. Why should ostrich and rabbit (very healthy meats) not be *kosher*, while chicken and duck are *kosher*? Why should shark and catfish not be *kosher*, while salmon and tuna are *kosher*? The health theory does not seem to be an overall adequate explanation for *kashrut*.

Jewishness. When reminded of your Jewishness, Jewish values will hopefully be a part of all aspects of your life.

So what are the laws of *kashrut*? The laws of *kashrut* can be broken down into several major categories:

(1) Animal species that are forbidden to eat;
(2) Parts of the animal that are forbidden to eat;
(3) Laws regarding how to slaughter animals;
(4) A prohibition against mixing meat and dairy products together; and,
(5) Laws regarding foods that cannot be eaten during the holiday of Passover (*Pesach*).

There are other categories outside of these five, but these five cover the major themes. What follows is a very brief description of the categories so that you can understand how the inventions described would make it easier to keep *kosher*.

Forbidden Animals

To be *kosher*, land animals (mammals) must have two characteristics: 1) a cloven (split) hoof and 2) chew its cud (Leviticus 11:3-8).[17] Animals from the waters must also have two characteristics, fins and scales (Leviticus 11:9-12).[18] For birds, there is no general rule, but the *Torah* lists 24 birds that are not *kosher* in Deuteronomy 12:14-18. Presumably all other birds are *kosher*. However, because the exact species mentioned in the *Torah* are not known with 100% certainty, unless there has been a continuing tradition of the bird being

---

[17] Examples of *kosher* mammals include cow, deer, lamb, and goat, while examples of *treif* mammals include pig, rabbit, dog, camel, horse, and bear.
[18] Examples of *kosher* animals from the water include tuna, salmon, and herring, while examples of *treif* animals from the water include crab, lobster, shrimp, shark, and catfish.

kosher, the bird is not considered *kosher*.[19] All reptiles, amphibians and insects are not *kosher*, except for four species of locusts mentioned in the *Torah*. Because we are no longer certain which locust species the *Torah* allows Jews to eat, all Jewish communities (except for the Yemenites) prohibit eating any locust. So if you happen to have a hankering for some delicious locusts, please find a local Yemenite rabbi to help you pick the right ones.

Forbidden Animal Parts

A Jew may not consume the blood of an animal. (Leviticus 17:10). To remove the blood so that you do not violate this prohibition, the blood is drained from the animal after slaughter. After the blood is drained, the flesh of the animal is coated in salt to absorb the remaining surface blood. The salt is then washed off the animal. This practice of salting the flesh to remove blood is why *kosher* meat often tastes saltier than non-*kosher* meat. In addition to the prohibition of consuming blood, the sciatic nerve and nearby blood vessels are forbidden. This prohibition derives from the story in Genesis where Jacob's hip socket is injured during his fight with G-d (or an angel of G-d). To commemorate this event, Jews do not eat meat containing the sciatic nerve. Lastly, a specific kind of fat called *chelev*, which surrounds the liver and other vital organs, is also forbidden. (Leviticus 7:32).

Kosher Slaughtering

Before and after slaughtering, an animal must be examined to determine whether it is healthy because the meat from a diseased animal is not *kosher*. After examination, a highly trained individual called a *shochet* kills the animal in a

---

[19] Examples of *kosher* birds include chicken, duck, goose, and turkey, while examples of *treif* birds include ostrich, vulture, raven, swan, eagle, and stork.

proscribed manner. The actual act of slaughtering involves cutting the trachea, esophagus, carotid arteries, jugular veins and vagus nerves in a single swift action using a knife having no imperfections. In some community traditions, there is an additional step of examining the lungs of an animal after slaughter. If the lungs are smooth (which is indicative of a healthy animal), the meat is said to be *glatt kosher*. If the lungs are not smooth and have adhesions, the animal is not *glatt kosher*.

Prohibition Against Mixing Meat and Dairy Products

The prohibition against not eating meat and dairy products together comes from several verses in the *Torah*. The *Torah* forbids "boiling a kid [goat/cow/sheep] in its mother's milk." (Exodus 23:10; 34:26, and Deuteronomy 14:21). This prohibition has been interpreted broadly to not only prohibit cooking meat and milk together but eating them together, using plates that have touched both milk and meat, or even using an oven that has cooked both milk and meat products if the oven has not been *kashered* in between uses.[20]

Not eating milk and meat together is not just about the simultaneous consumption of milk and meat products (such as would be the case in eating a something like a cheeseburger). There must be a separation of time between eating milk and meat products. Different communities, even amongst the Orthodox, have different standards for how long you should wait before eating dairy after eating meat. Some traditions only require only a one-hour separation, while others require up to a six-hour separation. Authorities are less strict for the amount of separation time required for eating meat after dairy.

---

[20] The act of making an item *kosher* for use is called "kashering" or "koshering," and the item that has undergone this process is said to have been "kashered."

Foods that are neither meat nor dairy are said to be *pareve*, which means *neutral*. Examples of *pareve* foods include fruits, vegetables, eggs, and fish. There are no restrictions for mixing *pareve* foods with milk or meat products. [21]

Kosher for Passover (*Pesach*)

The holiday of *Pesach* commemorates the Hebrews quickly leaving slavery in Egypt. The Hebrews had to leave Egypt so quickly that they did not have time for their bread to rise. To remember and relive this experience, Jews do not eat *chametz*. *Chametz* are five grain species mentioned in the *Torah* that G-d specifically forbid Jews from eating on *Pesach*. These grains are: wheat, oats, rye, barley, and spelt. A Jew can only eat these grains during *Pesach* if they are in the form of *matzah*, which is a brittle cracker baked without yeast (so the product does not rise with baking). *Matzah* is the bread product that would have been eaten as the Hebrews quickly escaped slavery. Ashkenazi Jews of Eastern European descent prohibit other food items called *kitniyot* (e.g., corn, rice, beans). Since the appearance of *kitniyot* can often be confused with *chametz*, especially if the *kitniyot* are ground into flour, Ashkenazi Jews prohibit their consumption as a safeguard against accidentally eating *chametz*. Sephardic Jews (not from Eastern Europe, but from the Mediterranean and Middle East) do not have the tradition of prohibiting *kitniyot* during *Pesach*.

Kashrut Patents

The following 22 patents relate to various aspects of *kashrut*, such as slaughtering, using alternative dairy/meat products, and *kashering* utensils, containers, and ovens.

---

[21] Although Jews understand that fish is a "meat" in the scientific sense, it is not the category of meat that requires any separation from dairy products. Some individuals have a tradition of not mixing fish with other meat products, but this is not derived from any *Torah* or *Talmud* prohibition.

Automated Machine and Related Methods for Seasoning Meat

U.S. Patent Number: 7,597,062

Inventors: Keith Fetterhoof and Cloyd Bowsman

Date Issued: October 6, 2009

Problem: The *Torah* prohibits consumption of blood. Leviticus 7:26 states, "And ye shall eat no manner of blood, whether it be of bird or of beast, in any of your dwellings." To abide by this commandment and remove surface blood on the animal, the inside and outside of a slaughtered animal is covered in large-grained "kosher salt," which absorbs blood. The salting process for koshering meat can be laborious and time-consuming, so is there a way to automate the salting process?

How the Problem is Solved: The inventors created a machine to automate the kosher salting of poultry. The machine has a conveyor mechanism, a seasoning projecting mechanism, a blower, and a paddle to sweep the salt toward the poultry.

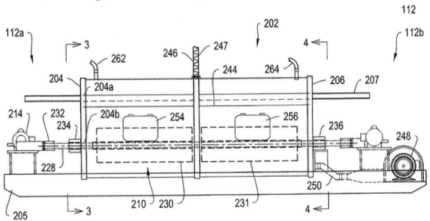

Feather-Removing Apparatus

U.S. Patent Number: 1,660,659

Inventors: Alexander Vermes et al.

Date Issued: February 28, 1928

Problem: If you have ever compared store-bought *kosher* chickens with store-bought non-*kosher* chickens you may have noticed that the *kosher* chickens have more feathers intact on the skin compared to non-*kosher* chickens. This is because non-*kosher* chickens are soaked in warm water, which makes it easier to remove the feathers. *Kosher* chickens cannot be soaked in warm water before de-feathering because soaking in warm water would be akin to cooking the chicken before the chicken has become *kosher* by going through the *kashering* process, such as salting. Feathers are not as easy to pluck using cold water, thus *kosher* chickens are left with more feathers intact. Is there a way to remove more feathers on a *kosher* bird?

How the Problem is Solved: This invention is for a device that holds a tightly pressed lower comb that rapidly hits a bar that plucks the comparatively strong resisting feathers off the chicken without cutting the feathers.

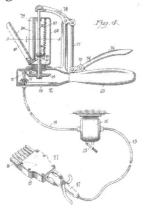

Food Preparation Facilitator Apparatus

Patent Number: 5,632,510

Inventor: Arthur Morowitz

Date Issued: May 27, 1997

Problem: How do you keep a restaurant kitchen informed of your *kosher* diet restrictions? Yes, you can tell the waiter that you only eat kosher food, don't eat pork, don't mix dairy and meat products, but you might be playing a game of telephone with the waiter, and the chef may not get it right.

How the Problem is Solved: This invention is for a kit that includes a series of cards that contain internationally recognized dietary restriction symbols. The inventor specifically mentions "kosher only" cards a part of his invention.

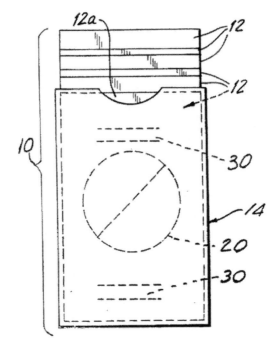

Cheese Substitutes

European Patent Number: 1,494,540

Inventor: Frederick Wade Mussawir-Key

Date Issued: January 12, 2005

Problem: Let's say you want some spaghetti and meatballs covered in Parmesan cheese. If you keep *kosher*, you can't have the meatball and cheese together because of the prohibition of mixing dairy and meat products. There are several options, some of which include using either fake meat or non-dairy cheese.

How the Problem is Solved: There are many patents for meat substitutes and non-dairy cheeses. In this invention, the inventor created a cheese substitute "comprising 60-95% bland edible particulate, 1-25% vegetable fat component, 1-15% salt component and parmesan flavouring." One form of the edible particulate is soy flour. The combination of parmesan flavoring that comes from a non-dairy source, with a specific percent of edible particulate, and specific percent vegetable fat and salt, give this fake parmesan cheese the appearance and taste of real parmesan cheese (at least according to the inventor).

Beef and Vegetable Extract

U.S. Patent Number: 994,885

Inventor: Nathan Sulzberger

Date Issued: June 13, 1911

Problem: Since dairy and meat cannot be mixed together, there is a need for meat substitutes when an observant Jew wants to eat foods that are traditionally made from meat. There are several meat substitutes and this patent is directed to a substitute beef extract that can be used with dairy products.

How the Problem is Solved: The inventor claims "an extract to be used in the preparation of bouillon, gravies, and sauces, consisting of peptonized albumin of vegetable origin, suitably seasoned, flavored and spiced, and containing fat." Albumin is a type of protein that is commonly found in egg whites, but also found in plants and fungi. To peptonize is to convert a protein into a peptone (a mixture of polypeptides and amino acids), essentially a digested, broken down protein. The inventor discloses that mushrooms can be used in this beef substitute extract. The mushrooms are heated in water and the resultant liquid is thickened like gravy after the liquid is boiled off.

Gelatin Substitute Product and Uses in Food Preparation

U.S. Patent Number: 8,932,660

Inventors: Philippe Bertrand and Philippe Marand

Date Issued: January 13, 2015

Problem: Gelatin in food products is problematic for Jews who keep *kosher* because most gelatins are derived from animal bones. For gelatin to be *kosher*, it must come from a *kosher* animal killed in a *kosher* manner, or the gelatin can be non-animal based.

How the Problem is Solved: There are numerous patents for non-animal based gelatin. In this one, the gelatin "consists of at least 99% weight cocoa butter, deodorized to an extent of 90-95%, and is in the form of a powder."

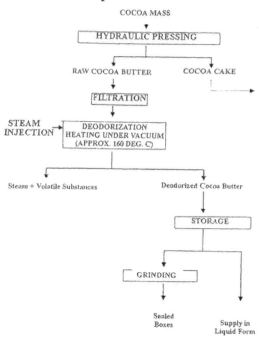

Quinoa-Based Beverages and Method of Creating Quinoa-Based Beverages

European Patent Number: 2,670,833

Inventor: Joseph Kamelgard

Date Issued: December 11, 2013

Problem: During the holiday of *Pesach* (Passover), Jews are prohibited from eating five types of grains called *chametz*. These grains are wheat, barley, spelt, rye and oats. Ashkenazi Jews (Jews of Eastern European descent) also have additional strictures where eating beans, rice, corn, lentils, and some other products called *kitniyot* are prohibited. These prohibitions make drinking beer nearly impossible during Passover. So what should you do if you want a beer during Passover?

How the Problem is Solved: This invention is for brewing a quinoa-based alcoholic beverage. Quinoa is not one of the five prohibited grains or *kitniyot*, yet quinoa has grain-like properties. Normally quinoa would have an unpleasant flavor if made into a drink, but the inventor came up with a way to make great tasting quinoa beer. First, quinoa is malted into an extract, then boiled, cooled to about 20-26°C and placed in an air-locked vessel. There are several optional steps listed, such as kilning the quinoa, mashing the malted quinoa, and lautering the wort. In the end, you have a *kosher* for Passover beer.

Kosher Meat-Based Pet Food Products

U.S. Patent Number: 6,277,435

Inventors: Martine Lacombe and Marc Michels

Date Issued: August 21, 2001

Problem: Although pets are not required to keep *kosher*, many religious families do not want to bring non-kosher products into their home but still want their pets to have a healthy meat-based diet.

How the Problem is Solved: This invention is for a pet food composition that is "from about 15 to 50 weight percent of kosher meat wherein the kosher meat is from a healthy animal, is washed in cold water and salted, said composition further comprising a source of carbohydrates, a source of fiber, a source of fat and at least 2.44% omega-6 fatty acids and at least 0.49% omega-3 fatty acids." Even non-Jews who would like to feed their pet a meat-based diet, but want the peace of mind that the meat in their pet food didn't come from animals that died from disease may have an interest in kosher pet foods.

FIG. 2

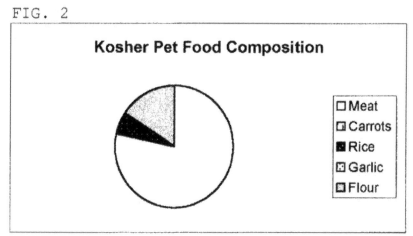

Bake-Oven

U.S. Patent Number: 1,169,555

Inventors: Behr Manischewitz et al.

Date Issued: January 25, 1916

Problem: In order for *matzah* to be *kosher*, specific guidelines must be followed (especially regarding the maximum amount of time allowed to bake *matzah*) or else the *matzah* may not be consumed during *Pesach*. Is there a way to ensure that all *matzah* is consistently baked correctly according to Jewish law?

How the Problem is Solved: This invention is for a *matzah*-baking oven. The oven has main walls, a longitudinal series of transverse, independently-partitioned firing-chambers within the main walls, and a longitudinal tunneled baking-chamber provided within the main walls. An independent iron structure is arranged in heating-relation with the firing-chambers.

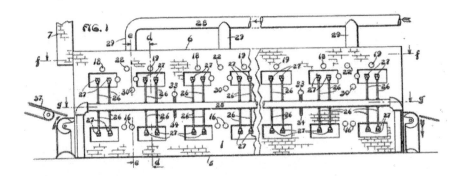

Fish Gelatinous Composition for Use as an Ingredient in Tablets

U.S. Patent Number: 6,423,346

Inventors: Morten Mohr Hansen et al.

Date Issued: July 23, 2002

Problem: Gelatin is often used in tablets, but gelatin is problematic for Jews for two reasons. Most gelatin comes from cow bones so *kosher* gelatin must come from a cow that has been slaughtered in a *kosher* manner, and you cannot have dairy after eating meat-based gelatin. By merely ingesting a gelatin tablet made from meat gelatin, you are restricting what you can eat for several hours. Since there are no restrictions for mixing fish with dairy, the use of fish gelatin has advantages for the observant Jew. However, fish gelatin does not have the same structural properties as cow gelatin and there have been reported difficulties in using fish gelatin for forming tablets. The inventors contend that fish gelatin normally has insufficient strength to resist the mechanical forces used during tablet creation. Is there a way to overcome the problems of fish gelatin?

How the Problem is Solved: The inventors have created a fish gelatinous composition with high mechanical strength so that it can be used as an ingredient in tablets, such as nutritional supplements. The composition includes a fish gelatinous protective colloid containing at least 50% by weight of fish gelatin and created by a particle forming spray congelation method or a double emulsifying method.

Low Density Marshmallow-Like Products and Methods of Producing the Same

U.S. Patent Number: 6,376,003

Inventor: James Cross

Date Issued: April 23, 2002

Problem: Most marshmallows contain gelatin, thus making them *treif* because marshmallow producers generally do not use *kosher* gelatin in making their marshmallows. *Treif* marshmallows prevent an appreciable number of potential Jewish consumers from purchasing products containing marshmallows. But what if marshmallows could be made without gelatin at all?

How the Problem is Solved: This invention is for a composition and method of making dehydrated marshmallows, like the kind found in cereals such as Lucky Charms. The mixture is not made from any gelatin or animal product but is a "mixture being essentially gelatin-free and comprising from about 69%-80% by weight sugar, from about 6-12% by weight water, protein flour and at least one chemical gassing agent selected from the group consisting of sodium bicarbonate, monocalcium phosphate and sodium aluminum phosphate, said percentages based upon the total weight of the mixture taken as 100% by weight, said mixture having a dough-like consistency capable of being rolled into stampable, thin sheets."

Animal Hold Down/Neck Stretcher for Kosher Slaughter on a Double-Rail Animal Support System (1)

U.S. Patent Number: 3,979,792

Inventors: Ralph P. Prince et al.

Date Issued: September 14, 1976

Problem: The *shochet* who slaughters an animal needs clear access to the jugular vein and other anatomical structures in order to kill the animal in a *kosher* manner. Access to the neck to ensure proper slaughter can be difficult in a live moving animal. Are there apparatuses that can position the animal easier for *kosher* slaughtering?

How the Problem is Solved: One way to gain clear access to the jugular vein is to stretch the neck of a cow through the use of a jaw holder. In this invention, instead of using a jaw holder, this assembly has a triangular shoulder brace that fits over the shoulder of the animal, sufficient to keep the neck of the animal stretched. A spring secures the head of the cow beneath the ears and adjusts to the size of the animal's head. A shoulder brace also prevents any friction from developing between the frame and the side walls by preventing the animal from slipping through the back frame.

FIG.2

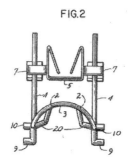

Adam L. Diament

Animal Hold Down/Neck Stretcher for Kosher Slaughter on a Double-Rail Animal Support System (2)

U.S. Patent Number: 3,967,343

Inventors: Westervelt et al.

Date Issued: July 6, 1976

Problem: The neck of a cow needs to be stretched in order to have clear access to the jugular vein for *kosher* slaughtering. (See previous page). Are there other apparatuses and methods that would make *kosher* slaughter easier?

How the Problem is Solved: In this invention, there are pair of parallel outer bars, a circular shaped cross bar, another pair of parallel holding bars, a jaw holder connected to the unconnected ends of the parallel holding bars, flexible double strips to hold the neck, and an outwardly extended bearing connected to the outer bars for holding the frame of the assembly on the back of the animal. Below is a figure of the sequence of placing the patented device on the animal, and removing the animal from the device after slaughter.

FIG.5

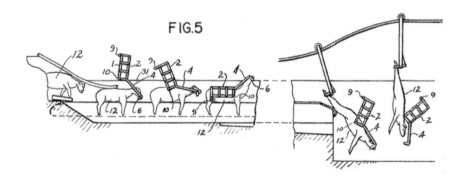

80

Apparatus and Method of Slaughtering Large Domestic Animals

U.S. Patent Number: 6,083,094

Inventor: Zachariha Cohen

Date Issued: July 4, 2000

Problem: Animals must be fully conscious when killed in order to be *kosher*. It is often difficult to restrain and handle large animals, such as cattle, that are fully conscious before slaughter. Can a device be used to make it easier to restrain these large animals?

How the Problem is Solved: This invention claims an apparatus for an animal enclosure that is mounted to a base. The base can rotate around a longitudinal axis so that the animal can be inverted for slaughtering. The apparatus has an opening near the bottom for access to the hooves so that when the animal is turned upside down, the animal can be shackled near its hooves. This apparatus minimizes the possibility of injury to the operator during the shackling. There are also provisions for holding and stretching out the neck of the animal.

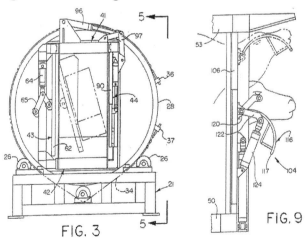

FIG. 3

FIG. 9

Double-Rail Animal Securing Assembly

U.S. Patent Number: 3,997,940

Inventors: Ralph P. Prince et al.

Date Issued: December 21, 1976

Problem: Restraining a large animal, such as a cow, and positioning the cow so that the neck is in the proper position for *kosher* slaughtering can be difficult. What other devices can be used to make it easier to slaughter an animal?

How the Problem is Solved: In this invention, there are two sets of parallel rails to hold the animal and neck in position. The four legs of the cow straddle the two rails, and the body rests on the rails. The back of the device holds the rump and back securely to the rails. The assembly also has structures to restrain and stretch the neck upward for ritual slaughter.

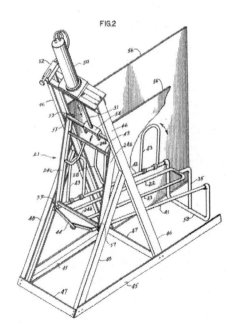

Apparatus for Slaughtering in Accordance with Hallal or Kosher Provisions

U.S. Patent Number: 4,308,638

Inventor: Akiel Senussi

Date Issued: January 5, 1982

Problem: The inventor contends that prior to his invention, tables used to hold animals for slaughter were too low for the slaughterer to stand comfortably while cutting the jugular vein of the cow. The tables were not conducive for large scale slaughtering procedures, and in addition, the means to collect the animal's blood was inefficient.

How the Problem is Solved: This invention is for an apparatus that has a table top with a concave surface and a drainage system at the lower portion of the table to allow blood to drain away from the animal. The apparatus also has several straps to restrain the animal's legs, torso and head. Also included is a latch to release the animal after it has been slaughtered.

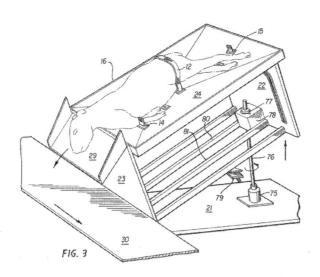

FIG. 3

Determining Respiratory or Circulatory Health Condition in Animals for Improved Management

U.S. Patent Number: 7,670,292

Inventor: John Haynes

Date Issued: March 2, 2010

Problem: One of the requirements for an animal to be *kosher* is that it must be healthy before slaughter. Some Jews have a tradition of only eating meat if the slaughtered animal has undergone a specific lung inspection to look for any lung adhesions. Smooth lungs indicate a healthy animal, while lungs with adhesions indicate a sick animal (and would not be *kosher*). Animals that pass this lung inspection test are said to be *glatt kosher*. The Yiddish word *glatt* means *smooth* in English and relates to the smooth lungs of a healthy animal. This inspection can be time consuming, but can the inspection be sped up somehow?

How the Problem is Solved: This invention is for an ultrasound device to determine whether the lungs look healthy. This device would not replace manual inspection of the lungs, but may speed up the process by eliminating manual inspection of animals that fail the ultrasound test.

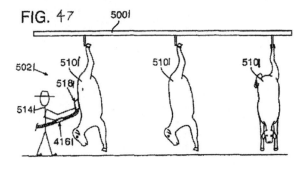

FIG. 47

Process of Koshering Containers (1)

U.S. Patent Number: 4,830,675

Inventor: Howard Skolnik

Date Issued: May 16, 1989

Problem: Containers must be *kashered* if the container has ever been in contact with food that might not have been *kosher*, or has been in contact with both milk and meat products. Some Jews *kasher* new pots and pans even if they are brand new. *Kashering* pots and pans can be fairly simple if the pots and pans are small, but for big drums used to transport large volumes of food, kashering can be more difficult.

How the Problem is Solved: The inventor, Howard Skolnik, received several patents for *kashering* containers. He describes methods that includes steps of washing the interior of the container, rinsing the interior with a water wash, applying a rust-inhibiting substance, and removing oil or other contaminants from the pores of the surfaces by exposing the surface to a flame in excess of 400 degrees for at least two minutes. Optionally, a coating made from *kosher* ingredients can be applied to the surface, and the coating is cured when exposed to the flame.

Process of Koshering Containers (2)

U.S. Patent Number: 4,906,301

Inventor: Howard Skolnik

Date Issued: March 6, 1990

Problem: See "Process of Koshering Containers (1)."

How the Problem is Solved: Continuing from his previous invention, Skolnik describes a method for koshering large food storage containers by using specific steps of washing, rinsing, removing contaminants by a flame, applying an epoxy/phenolic composition containing no non-*kosher* ingredients, and applying heat to the interior to cure the epoxy coat.

Process of Koshering Containers (3)

U.S. Patent Numbers: 5,026,431

Inventors: Howard Skolnik, Paul Dukes Jr. and Jonah Gerwitz

Date Issued: June 25, 1991

Problem: When storing foods in containers, the entire container must be made kosher, including the walls of the container. This can be difficult and time consuming without automation.

How the Problem is Solved: Here, Skolnik patents another method of *kashering* metallic food storage containers by using two different flame-burners for removing oils, grease and other contaminants on the interior and exterior surfaces, as shown in the illustration below.

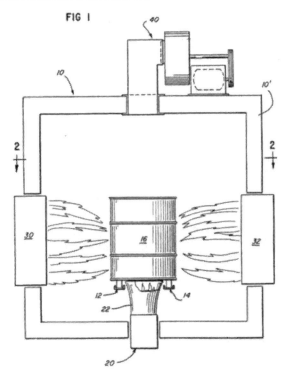

FIG I

Process and Apparatus for Koshering Container Lids (1)

U.S. Patent Number: 5,024,597

Inventor: Howard Skolnik and Jonah Gerwitz

Date Issued: June 18, 1991

Problem: When storing or cooking foods, the entirety of the container must be *kosher*, including the lids of pots and pans. Is there an automated way to *kasher* lids?

How the Problem is Solved: Exposing an item to fire is one way of *kashering* it. In this invention, the inventor created a new type of housing that encloses a conveyor system. The lids pass through the housing where they are flame treated on two sides simultaneously, as shown by the illustration below.

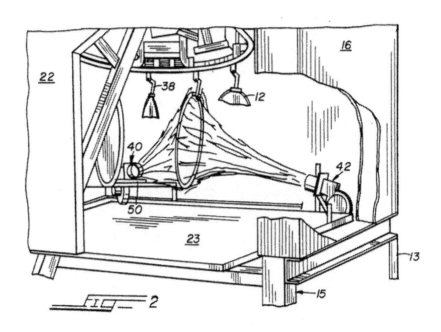

Process and Apparatus for Koshering Container Lids (2)

U.S. Patent Number: 5,034,067

Inventors: Jonah Gerwitz, Howard Skolnik, and Paul Dukes

Dates Issued: June 23, 1991

Problem: When storing foods in a container, the entirety of the container must be *kosher*, including the interior and exterior surface of the storage container.

How the Problem is Solved: Part of this patent includes an oven-apparatus for flaming the interior and exterior surfaces of containers. Containers are conveyed through a tunnel in the main housing. Inside the housing the containers are subjected to vertical and horizontal flame-burners mounted to the apparatus. The conveyor can lift and rotate the containers as they pass through so that all surfaces are *kashered*.

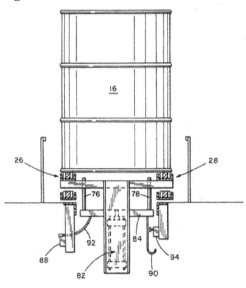

FIG. 5

Chapter 5
Food and Beverage Patents

In the Introduction, I discussed that for many people who identify as being Jewish, being Jewish is not about having a particular faith or practicing Jewish observance, but is cultural.

Jewish culture includes song, dance, celebrating holidays, having a Jewish social circle, participating in Jewish life cycle events, and of course, eating Jewish foods.

Since Jews come from all over the world, there actually is no common Jewish cuisine. European Jews have a very different cuisine from Persian Jews, who have a very different cuisine from Indian Jews, who have a different cuisine from Ethiopian Jews. In America, most Jews come from an Ashkenazi background (Eastern European), and their cuisine comes from Eastern Europe, so if you ask someone in America what Jewish food is, that person will probably list some Ashkenazi Jewish foods.

Commonly associated foods with Ashkenazi Jews are: bagels, lox (smoked salmon), *kreplach* (dumplings), *kneidlach* (*matzah* balls), *latkes* (potato pancakes), herring, gefilte fish, pickles, *borscht*, *kugel*, *cholent*, *knishes*, *kishkes*, *pierogis*, chopped liver, stuffed cabbage, and *tzimmes*.

Sephardic Jews,[22] Mizrahi Jews,[23] and Persian Jews have an entirely different cuisine. Their cuisines emphasize more salads, stuffed vegetables, lentils, dried fruits, lamb, ground beef, and include dishes called *chreime, chamin, sambusak, falafel,* and *tabbouleh.* The spices used in the various Jewish cuisines from around the world also differ dramatically depending on the local spices available.

Despite the different cuisines, there are a few common staples. All Jews will prepare a type of bread called *challah* for *Shabbat,* though how *challah* is made is different among the different Jewish communities. Jews will also all eat *matzah* on Passover. Most of the patent applications related to Jewish foods are directed toward *challah,* bagels, and *matzah.*

---

[22] Jews whose ancestors came from Spain, but were scattered throughout Africa, the Mediterranean and the Middle East after their expulsion in 1492.

[23] Jews whose ancestors are from the Middle East are known as Mizrahi Jews. There is a fair amount of overlap of traditions between Sephardic Jews and Mizrahi Jews, so the terms are often conflated, though there are numerous differences between Mizrahi Jewish traditions and Sephardic Jewish traditions.

Bagel Slicers

U.S. Patent Number: 3,338,282

Inventor: Paul Blum

Date Issued: August 29, 1967

Problem: Bagels are difficult to slice down the middle because they don't stand upright by themselves. Most people cut a bagel by holding it in one hand as they carefully slice the bagel with a knife held in the other hand. This practice is dangerous and has landed many people in the hospital. Bagel slicing is actually the fifth most dangerous activity in the American kitchen.[24] Many bagel-slicing devices have been patented; here is one of the first patented bagel slicers.

How the Problem is Solved: Clamping cups hold a bagel in place. A knife is attached to a vertical member and pivots down to cut the bagel between the clamps, as illustrated below.

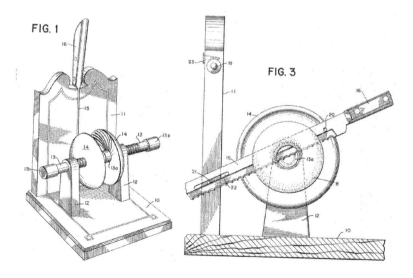

---

[24] http://freakonomics.com/2009/11/30/bagel-danger/

Bagel Slicer

U.S. Patent Number: 3,347,296

Inventor: Alex Rothman

Date Issued: October 17, 1967

Problem: See previous page of "Bagel Slicers."

How the Problem is Solved: In this early bagel slicing patent, the bagel is placed in the middle of two circular depressions. The bagel is held between two plates hinged together, but allows a knife to slice in-between the two plates. You hold the device by the handles and do not need to hold the bagel directly when you slice it.

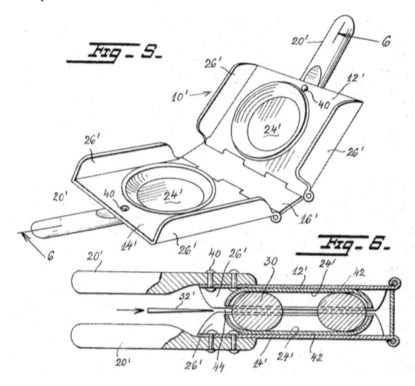

Process for Making Frozen Bagel Shapes

U.S. Patent Number: 5,707,676

Inventor: Ronald Savelli

Date Issued: January 13, 1998

Problem: According to the inventor, using pre-frozen bagel dough is not as good as using fresh dough for making bagels. Frozen dough does not rise as well as fresh dough, and the crust of the bagel is too thin. Also, bagels made from frozen dough tend to become misshapen and form blisters when baked. Is there a way you can use frozen bagel dough while avoiding all these problems?

How the Problem is Solved: To solve these problems, the inventor bathes the bagel dough pieces "in an aqueous food grade acidic solution warmed to a temperature up to about 190 degrees" before freezing the bagel. This purportedly solves the problems associated with using frozen bagel dough.

Filled Bagel Dough Product and Method

U.S. Patent Number: 5,236,724

Inventor: Alvin Burger

Date Issued: August 17, 1993

Problem: One of the most common things to eat with a bagel is cream cheese. But cream cheese can get messy when spread in the normal way on the flat side of a cut bagel. Is there a way to make and eat a bagel with cream cheese without causing a mess?

How the Problem is Solved: This invention is for a filled bagel dough product and a method of making the product. First, the dough is made into a hollow ball. Cream cheese is placed in the cavity of the ball. The dough is sealed around the cream cheese and then the product is steamed (rather than boiled) and then baked.

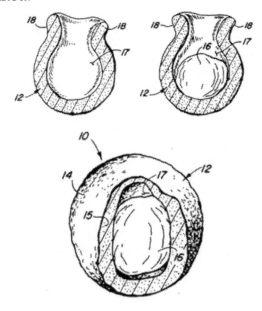

Dough Embossing Apparatus

U.S. Patent Number: 3,936,255

Inventor: Joseph Bellacicco

Date Issued: February 3, 1976

Problem: During the traditional Friday night *Shabbat* meal, several prayers are recited. One prayer thanks G-d for bringing forth bread from the earth (the prayer is called the *motzi*). The type of bread traditionally eaten on *Shabbat* is called *challah*, which is often braided and made from eggs, flour, water, sugar, yeast and salt. But what if you are horrible at braiding? How can you make a decent looking *challah*?

How the Problem is Solved: This invention is an embossing apparatus that presses dough into a particular shape so that the bread looks like it has been braided. The apparatus includes an endless belt that receives dough and transports the dough though an embossing wheel that creates a braided shape.

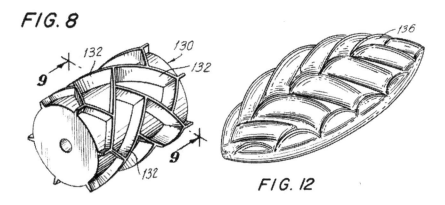

FIG. 8

FIG. 12

Method and Apparatus for Producing Braided Baked Products

U.S. Patent Number: 5,637,341

Inventor: Ram Rivlin

Date Issued: June 10, 1997

Problem: So far we've seen a way to make *challah* look like it has been braided, even when it hasn't. But let's say you actually want to braid *challah* but don't know how, or you own *challah*-making factory and don't have the personnel to braid all the *challah*. Braiding *challah* may not take a long time if you make just one, but if you need to make hundreds, it would take a long time. What can you do?

How the Problem is Solved: This invention is for a device and a method where you first insert dough through a hole in the device. The device has die members that rotate, so that it interweaves the strips of dough into a braid to make braided *challah*.

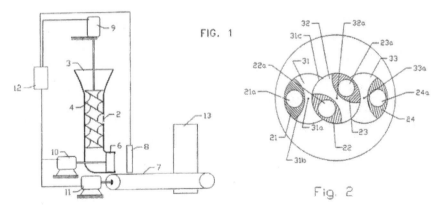

Frozen Challah Dough with Protrusion or Marking or Separated Piece for Observing the Mitzvah of Hafrashat Challah (Separating of Challah)

U.S. Patent Application Number: 13/919,023
(Patent Pending)

Inventor: Fischel Offman

Date Filed: June 17, 2013

Problem: The *Torah* says "Of the first of your dough you shall lift up a cake as an offering...from the first of your dough you shall give to the Lord an offering throughout your generations." (Numbers 15:20-21). From this verse, Jews in ancient times gave part of the *challah* dough to a priest (*kohen*). Today, since there is no Holy Temple from where the priests make sacrifices, it is common practice to burn the portion of bread that was traditionally given to the priest. But what if you don't want to mess up your beautifully braided *challah* by tearing off a piece?

How the Problem is Solved: This invention is for a specially molded frozen challah where there is a protruding piece specifically created to enable you to perform the commandment of removing the *challah* piece for the priest. This way, the protruding piece can be removed, but your *challah* still looks like a fully formed *challah*.

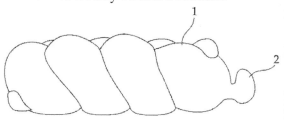

Distributor for Alcoholic Beverages

U.S. Patent Number: 5,484,002

Inventor: Michael Kupietzky

Date Issued: January 16, 1996

Problem: One of the prayers recited before the *Shabbat* meal is the blessing over the wine (*kiddush*). If you are having many guests over for dinner, or have a large gathering with hundreds of people, you many need to fill many cups of wine quickly and evenly without spilling. Is there a device that can help you out?

How the Problem is Solved: In this invention, wine or other beverages can be poured into a receptacle on top, and the wine will be distributed to goblets located under spouts. There have been many types of beverage distributors like this, but in this system, the wine receptacle can be flipped over when not in use, and act as a dust cover.

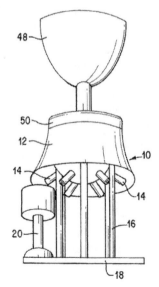

Tool for Treatment of a Substance on a Surface

U.S. Patent Number: 8,024,835

Inventor: Ayelet Hellerman

Date Issued: September 27, 2011

Problem: During the holiday of *Pesach* (Passover), Jews are prohibited from eating bread. Instead, Jews eat *matzah*, which is a brittle cracker-like product. It is nearly impossible to put any type of pressure on a piece of *matzah* without it breaking. Is there a special kind of knife that can be used to spread butter or cream cheese on *matzah* where the *matzah* will not break?

How the Problem is Solved: This invention is for a *matzah* spreader. The blade is made from a soft and bendable material so that when a certain amount of force is applied, the blade deflects (bends) to limit the amount of force exerted on the *matzah* so it won't break.

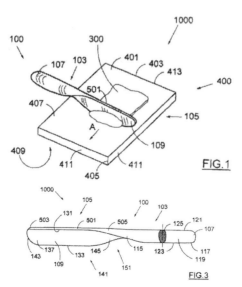

101

Weighing and Carton-Filling Device

U.S. Patent Number: 1,306,187

Inventor: Jacob Manischewitz

Date Issued: June 10, 1919

Problem: *Matzah* boxes are difficult to fill quickly due to its fragile nature. Is there a good way to quickly fill a box with *matzah* for transport?

How the Problem is Solved: Jacob Manischewitz (of the famous Manischewitz family) invented a three-sided container for *matzahs*. The heights of the sides of the container are shorter than the height of the *matzah*. The box is placed over the *matzah* and then flipped over. The three-sided container is then removed so that the *matzah* can now be placed in its filled shipping container. This device speeds up the entire *matzah* packaging process.

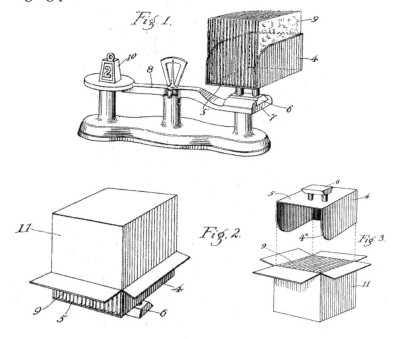

Method of Preparing an Edible Fish Product

U.S. Patent Number: 3,108,882

Inventor: Monroe Nash and Erich Freudenstein

Date Issued: October 29, 1963

Problem: Gefilte fish is a popular Jewish food, especially amongst Ashkenazi Jews. It is generally made from minced fish such as pike, whitefish and carp, and formed into a ball. Store-bought gefilte fish comes in a glass jar filled with many gefilte fish balls in a briny broth. It's commonly eaten on *Shabbat* and on *Pesach*. Historically there have been problems with making and storing gefilte fish. The flavors can leech out of the fish and the fish ball often crumbles in the broth.

How the Problem is Solved: This invention is for a method of preparing gefilte fish that has the steps of cooking the fish in a brine solution, flavoring the fish, and preparing a broth that has water, flavoring, and an edible gel from red seaweed. When made in this manner, the gefilte fish is resistant to decomposition at sterilization temperatures above 240 degrees.

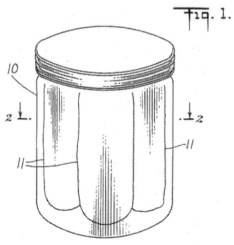

Fig. 1.

Chapter 6
Garment and
Ritual Item Patents

There are a number of garment-related items used in Jewish life. Many garments are worn as part of everyday Jewish attire while others are worn only at selected times. A Jewish prayer shawl (called a *tallit*) and its associated fringes called *tzitzit* have more patents associated with them than any other type of Jewish garment. There are also patents for *kippahs* (the Jewish head covering, called a *yarmulke* in Yiddish), and other ritualistic items such as *tefillin*, prayer breastplates, circumcision platforms, devices that help you honor the dead, and wedding memorabilia.

Multi Use Head Cover

U.S. Patent Number: 5,845,338

Inventor: Jeffrey Clark

Date Issued: December 8, 1998

Problem: During prayer services, Jewish men (and sometimes women) wear a head covering called a *kippah* (in Hebrew) or a *yarmulke* (in Yiddish). An Orthodox man wears a *kippah* the entire day. No one knows the exact origin of the *kippah*, but the *Talmud* states, "Cover your head in order that the fear of heaven may be upon you." (Shabbat 16b). One reason given for wearing a *kippah* is that it is a physical reminder of G-d's presence above you. Most *kippot* (plural of *kippah*) are fairly small, but there might be some situations where a small *kippah* is not practical, such as if you need to shade your eyes. How can a *kippah* shade your eyes? This inventor thought of a way.

How the Problem is Solved: This invention is for a detachable *kippah* that can fit inside of an adjustable visor (or baseball cap). The visor has interlocking plastic strips and a zipper to hold the *kippah* in place.

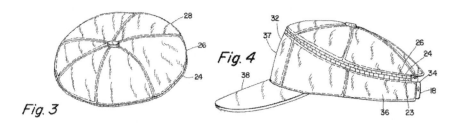

Fig. 3

Fig. 4

Combined Scarf and Prayer Shawl

U.S. Patent Number: 2,051,274

Inventor: Maurice Rubens

Date Issued: March 8, 1935

Problem: During certain prayer services, Jews wear a specific kind of a prayer shawl called a *tallit*. The *tallit* has *tzitzit* (fringes) on each of its four corners made up of knotted strings. The *tallit* and *tzitzit* together are a physical representation of the *Torah's* 613 commandments. In Hebrew, each letter is assigned a numerical value. In English, the equivalent would be that A=1, B=2, C=3, etc. The letters of the Hebrew word *tzitzit* add up to 600. When you add the eight strings and five knots of each tassel, the total is 613. But what if you want to wear a *tallit* but don't want the fringes exposed?

How the Problem is Solved: This invention is for a *tallit* that has a pocket on each of its four corners so the *tzitzit* can be tucked in. The *tallit* will look more like a regular shawl instead of a religious garment, and the *tzitzit* will be protected.

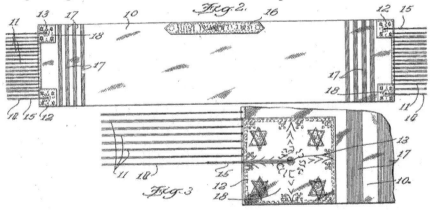

Tzitzit Garment

U.S. Patent Number: 8,756,712

Inventor: Tamir Goodman

Date Issued: June 24, 2014

Problem: As described earlier, a *tallit* is a religious garment with fringes (*tzitzit*) on the corners. Wrapping yourself with the garment serves as a reminder of the *Torah's* commandments. Most Orthodox men not only wear the *tallit* during prayer services but also wear a smaller undergarment version of the *tallit* throughout the day. This undergarment is called a *tallit katan* (literally meaning "small *tallit*") and looks somewhat like an undershirt. This *tallit katan* is usually fairly loose, which can cause problems for observant Jewish athletes, where loose undergarments might become a hindrance to performance.

How the Problem is Solved: This invention is for a *tallit katan* that has an under layer and outer layer. The under layer is made from a compressible elastic material, and one version of the invention also includes shorts (for a sports uniform) that have grips to hold the *tzitzit*.

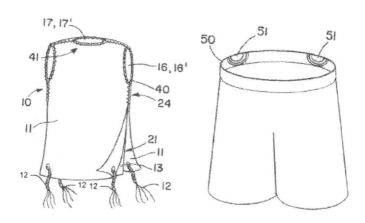

Tzitzioth Garment

U.S. Patent Number: 7,334,269

Inventor: Avraham Segol

Date Issued: February 26, 2008

Problem: As described previously, a *tallit katan* is an undergarment that has fringes (*tzitzit/tzizioth*) attached to the undergarment's four corners. Usually the undergarment drapes down and the sides are open, which may cause the garment to shift around in unwanted ways. Can the *tallit katan* still have open sides but wrap your torso in a better way?

How the Problem is Solved: In this invention, the *tallit katan* is about two-thirds open but has the appearance of being of being closed. If the *tallit katan* were completely closed and wrapped around the entire torso (like a t-shirt) then the *tallit katan* would not have the required four corners for *tzitzit* attachment. The inventor contends that the construction of his version of the *tallit katan* greatly reduces production costs.

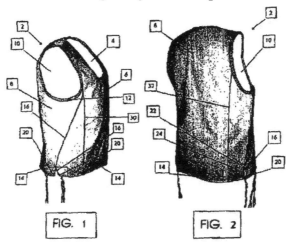

Garment with Retractable Fringes

U.S. Patent Number: 7,930,769

Inventor: Thomas Stern

Date Issued: April 26, 2011

Problem: As described previously, a *tallit* has *tzitzit* fringes that together represent the 613 commandments of the *Torah*. Sometimes the hanging *tzitzit* can get caught or snag on other objects. Is there a way to prevent the *tzitzit* from always hanging down and getting snagged?

How the Problem is Solved: This invention is for a *tallit* where the *tzitzit* can hang low during normal wear, such as during prayer services, but the *tallit* has a pocket with a retraction cord so that when you pull the retraction cord, the *tzitzit* can retract into the pocket.

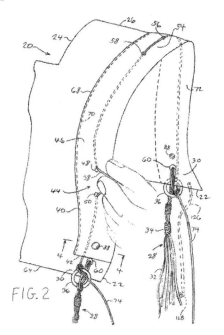

FIG. 2

Prayer Shawl Wedding Canopy

U.S. Patent Number: 5,227,215

Inventor: Rissa Sklar

Date Issued: July 13, 1993

Problem: A Jewish couple gets married under a canopy called a *chuppah*. The *chuppah* represents the couple's new home, which is open from all sides. Many *chuppahs* are made from a large *tallit* (prayer shall) with rods attached to each corner for holding the *chuppah* upright. Since a *tallit* can only be worn by one person during prayer services, is there a way that a *chuppah* can be made from two *tallitot*?

How the Problem is Solved: This invention is for a *chuppah* that is made from two separate *tallitot*. The *tallitot* are sewn together using a specific stitching described in the patent. The *chuppah* can be separated back into two separate *tallitot* after the wedding so the bride and groom can each have their own *tallit* made from their *chuppah*.

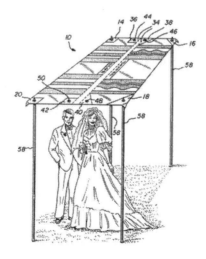

Prayer Breastplate

U.S. Patent Number: 8,627,513

Inventor: Bettie Colbert

Date Issued: January 14, 2014

Problem: During the times of the Holy Temple in Jerusalem, the Jewish people had a chief religious official called the *Kohen Gadol* (high priest). The high priest wore a special pocketed breastplate during his ceremonial duties. The breastplate was adorned with gems that symbolized the twelve tribes of Israel. Can a modern day prayer breastplate be devised for Jews to use today?

How the Problem is Solved: In this invention, the breastplate is made from a layered rectangular fabric interconnected along three perimeter edges to form an inner pocket. The breastplate has a looped portion to wear around your neck, ties to tie around your midsection, and the front surface is adorned with religious symbology.

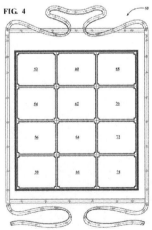

Protective Covers for Phylacteries

U.S. Patent Number: 8,789,690

Inventor: Ira Adler

Date Issued: January 14, 2014

Problem: Jewish men wear a set of phylacteries (called *tefillin* in Hebrew) during most weekday morning prayer services in accordance with the *Torah's* commandment to "Fix these words of mine in your hearts and minds; tie them as symbols on your hands and bind them on your foreheads." (Deuteronomy 11:18). Each *tefillin* includes a leather box that contains a short written portion from the *Torah*, and a knotted leather strap to wrap the box around the arm or head. To protect *tefillin* when not in use, the *tefillin* are placed in special protective covers. The knotted leather strap wraps around the cover. According to Rashi, a famous rabbi, the knot should not be placed under the *tefillin* when stored, but this can inadvertently happen when you wrap the straps around the protective cover. Is there a way that a protective cover can be made so that the knot always remains on top of the cover?

How the Problem is Solved: In this invention, the *tefillin* cover has an extra supplemental support surface specifically designed so that the knot always remains on the upper surface of the cover.

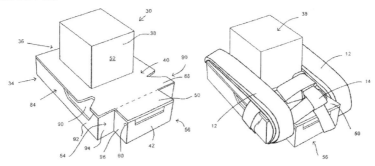

Bereavement Artifact

U.S. Patent Number: 8,438,764

Inventor: Howard Schiffman

Date Issued: May 14, 2013

Problem: When Jews visit the graves of loved ones, instead of placing flowers, Jews leave a stone to show respect. The exact origin of this tradition is unknown. However, if you want to leave something more than a stone, such as a letter or note, those items could cause problems for cemetery maintenance. Cemeteries frown upon leaving anything at a gravesite that can be blown away, even if secured in place. So how can you leave a note at your loved one's grave while complying with cemetery regulations?

How the Problem is Solved: This invention is for the combination of a rock having a compartment (similar to a hide-a-key) and biodegradable piece of paper made from cellulous-glycolic acid. The rock has an opening to allow in moisture from the outside. The paper (which can be a note to your deceased loved one) degrades quickly and stays within the rock so that it does not litter the cemetery.

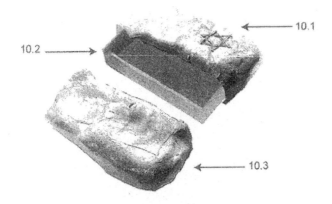

Earth Contact Burial Container, Burial Systems and Methods

U.S. Patent Number: 7,200,906

Inventors: Joseph Darst et al.

Date Issued: April 10, 2007

Problem: According to Jewish law, Jews should be buried within a day of death because the *Torah* says, "You shall bury him the same day...his body should not remain all night." (Deuteronomy 21:13). Jews are not cremated or embalmed because the *Torah* says, "You return to the soil, for from it you were taken. For you are dust and to dust you shall return." (Genesis 3:19). Because Jews should return to dust, coffins must be made of wood so they can decompose over time and allow the body to return to the soil. But is there a way to speed up the body returning to the soil?

How the Problem is Solved: In this specially designed coffin, there is an opening on the bottom panel of the coffin, so that when the coffin and body are lowered into the ground, the body comes into direct contact with the soil, which speeds up decomposition of the body.

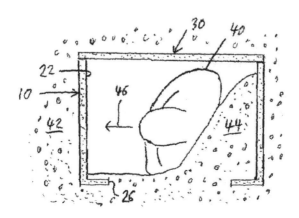

Adam L. Diament

Yahrzeit System and Method

U.S. Patent Number: 8,230,345

Inventors: Norman Rosenshein et al.

Date Issued: July 24, 2012

Problem: In Judaism, a deceased loved one is remembered not so much on his or her birth date, but on the anniversary of death, called a *yahrzeit*. There are various traditions associated with commemorating the yearly *yahrzeit*. One tradition is that a synagogue has a memorial wall with the names of synagogue members who have passed away. Often there are light bulbs next to each deceased person's name and the light bulbs are turned on during that person's *yahrzeit* month. However, with so many names and dates to remember, it can be difficult to keep track of everyone's *yarhzeit*. Is there a simple way to keep track?

How the Problem is Solved: This invention uses an electronic display connected to a network database that stores individuals' names, photos, and other information about the deceased.

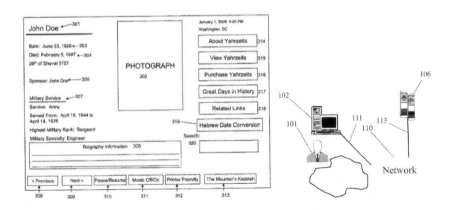

Pillow for Ritual Circumcisions and Method

U.S. Patent Number: 4,790,041

Inventor: Kiva Shtull

Date Issued: December 13, 1988

Problem: A Jewish boy is circumcised on his eighth day of life in a ceremony called *brit milah*, also known as a *bris*. The circumcision commandment is found in the book of Genesis, which says, "This is My covenant, which ye shall keep...And he that is eight days old shall be circumcised among you, every male throughout your generations." (Genesis 17:10-12). The person who circumcises the infant is called a *mohel*. In order to prevent any mishaps during circumcision, both the infant and *mohel* should be in comfortable positions. Is there a device that can be used so that the *mohel* has an easy time circumcising the boy?

How the Problem is Solved: This invention is for a pillow that has a lengthwise depression on top for the infant, and a perpendicular depression on the bottom that fits over the *mohel's* legs. The *mohel* can sit down, and lay the infant on top of the pillow in a stable manner so that both the pillow and infant are stabilized over the *mohel's* lap.

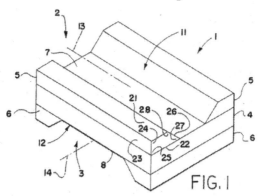

FIG. I

Wedding Glass Housing

U.S. Patent Number: 7,207,508

Inventor: Ephraim Golshevsky

Date Issued: April 24, 2007

Problem: One of the most iconic moments of a Jewish wedding is the breaking of the glass at the very end of the ceremony. There are many reasons given for this tradition. One of the more popular reasons is that even in a time a great joy, one should remember that there is sorrow and brokenness in the world. Many couples want a nice keepsake of the broken glass, but how do you best gather and keep the broken shards of glass?

How the Problem is Solved: This invention has a housing for a wine glass. The housing has a sheet that is puncture resistant and an intermediate layer that is compressible. When the groom stomps on the housing, the glass breaks, but the intermediate layer keeps the glass from leaving the housing. You are then left with a display box with the broken wedding glass.

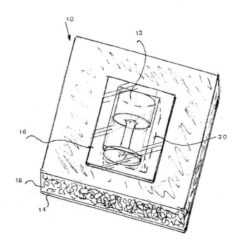

A Mikveh and
Method for Constructing Thereof

European Patent Number: 2,636,820

Inventor: Gidon Israel Ebenspanger

Date Issued: September 11, 2013

Problem: A *mikveh* is a Jewish ritual pool. Observant Jewish women go to a *mikveh* once a month, and men customarily go on various occasions, such as before getting married. Converts of both genders immerse themselves in a *mikveh* as part of the final step of conversion. Not every pool is *halachically* acceptable (i.e. in accordance with Jewish law) for use as a *mikveh*, and the specifications for a "kosher" *mikveh* can be difficult to conform to. How can a *mikveh* be easily constructed according to Jewish law?

How the Problem is Solved: There are scores, if not hundreds of laws for what makes a *mikveh* "kosher." Here, the inventor describes a series of steps (too many to list here) to construct a "kosher" *mikveh* using lightweight materials, instead of the traditional heavy materials.

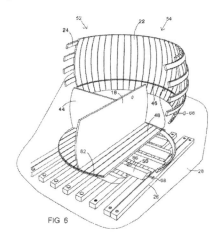

FIG 6

Chapter 7
Jewish Time
Management Patents

Classification of time is extremely important for the observant Jew. Jewish time and secular time are different in many respects. For example, the Jewish day does not begin at midnight, but begins and ends when the sun sets.

The Jewish year also is not as constant as the Gregorian calendar. Instead of 365 days (or 366 days in leap years), the Jewish year can have 353, 354, 355, 383, 384, or 385 days. The big fluctuation between 353 and 385 days is due to an extra <u>month</u> being added to the calendar seven times every 19 years in order to keep the holiday of Passover in the springtime, which the *Torah* requires. By adding in an extra month every few years, the solar and lunar cycles stay roughly in sync.

The Jewish month is based on the cycle of the moon and fluctuates between 29 and 30 days (since the moon's cycle is about 29.5 days). A specific month may have 29 days in one year, while in the next year it may have 30 days. To complicate matters, the Jewish year is not allowed to start on a Sunday, Wednesday, or Friday, so that the holiday of *Yom Kippur* does not fall on the day before or after *Shabbat*, and so another holiday, called *Hoshannah Rabbah*, does not fall on *Shabbat*.

In addition to the complexities of the year and months, Jewish time is also calculated differently within each day because the number of hours of daylight each day is different due to seasonal variations. These time calculations are called *zmanim*, and split the day into dawn, sunrise, midday, sunset, nightfall, and other splits of *halachic* significance. Splitting the day into the various *zmanim* is important because some ritual acts must be performed within certain timeframes of the day, and some prayers must be recited within certain timeframes as well. Since *zmanim* are calculated based on the sun's position relative to the individual, *zmanim* can be different even within the same zone. For example *zmanim* are different in Seattle, Washington, compared to *zmanim* in Los Angeles, California, even though both cities have exactly the same secular time.

The complexities of Jewish time have led to some pretty clever inventions for keeping track of the madness. Jewish time management is probably most important for determining when *Shabbat* begins and ends. *Shabbat* patents were described in their own chapter.

Electronic Hebrew Calendar and Date Calculator

U.S. Patent Number: 4,055,749

Inventor: Jonathan Kraushaar

Date Issued: October 25, 1977

Problem: The Hebrew calendar is very complicated. A year can be 353, 354, 355, 383, 384, or 385 days. The calendar follows a 19-year cycle where seven of the years have an extra month. There are still further complications regarding what day of the week a year is allowed to start on. With computers today, there is no problem converting the Hebrew calendar to the Gregorian calendar, but in 1976 (when this application was submitted), things weren't so easy.

How the Problem is Solved: This invention is for a device that accounts for all the complicated matters of the Jewish calendar and puts the calendar conversion into a "simple" electronic calendar device.

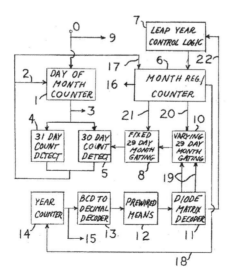

Calendar

U.S. Patent Number: 7,004,505

Inventor: Brad Perelman

Date Issued: February 28, 2006

Problem: Days in Judaism begin and end at sunset instead of the secular midnight-to-midnight timeframe. This causes a problem when trying to use an integrated Gregorian and Hebrew calendar because each Gregorian day covers two Hebrew days (one before sunset and one after sunset). Calendars that overlay Gregorian and Hebrew dates usually just indicate the Hebrew date before sunset and ignore the post-sunset date. Is there a way to make an integrated Gregorian/Hebrew calendar that accounts for the two Hebrew dates per single Gregorian date?

How the Problem is Solved: This invention is for a visually integrated calendar where the days are shown as two offset rectangles, one showing the Hebrew day, and the another showing the secular day, as shown below.

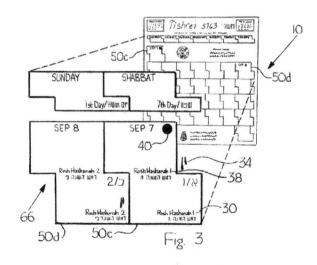

Fig. 3

Nonlinear Timer

U.S. Patent Number: 8,848,487

Inventor: Tidhar Eylon-Azoulay

Date Issued: September 30, 2014

Problem: The traditional secular clock measures all time increments equally. An hour is 60 minutes, no matter what. In Jewish time, an "hour" is 1/12 of the daylight time. Since the length of the day is measured by the course of the sun above the cap of the sky, referred to as the "diurnal arc" the Jewish "hour" changes throughout the year. Can there be a better clock for observant Jews than secular clocks to keep track of Jewish time and the *zmanim* in order to fulfill the various commandments associated with specific times of the day?

How the Problem is Solved: This invention is for a nonlinear timer/clock that keeps track of nonlinear Jewish time by calibrating it to a geographic position and time of year.

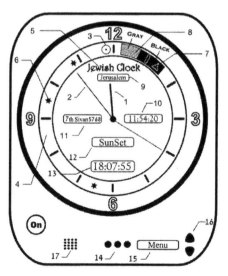

Figure 6

Shofar Timekeeping Apparatus and Method

U.S. Patent Number: 7,187,625

Inventor: Scott Riggi

Date Issued: March 6, 2007

Problem: Do you want an alarm clock, but are tired of the same old alarm sounds and the boring secular look?

How the Problem is Solved: This invention is for an alarm clock that includes a replica of a *shofar*.[25] Instead of a normal beeping or buzzing sound, the alarm clock plays the sounds that the *shofar* makes. In the author's opinion, of all the patents described in this book, this one is probably the least deserving of patent protection. A *shofar* sound from an alarm clock should not be patentable, anymore than an alarm clock that has sounds of dogs barking or cats meowing is patentable. A decorative *shofar* attached to the alarm clock likewise should not be patentable because the *shofar* on the alarm clock has no particular new function. Nevertheless, the patent office granted a patent for this device.

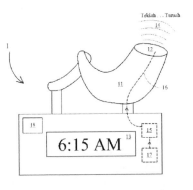

---

[25] A *shofar* is a musical instrument similar to a bugle but made from a ram's horn. Today, the most likely time to hear a *shofar* is during *Rosh Hashanah* and *Yom Kippur* services, or during the month of *Elul*, where the *shofar* is sounded every day during morning prayers.

Chapter 8
Miscellaneous Patents

Not every patent fits neatly into one of the previous categories, but still should be called a "Kosher Patent." Included in this chapter are a patent for detecting a genetic disease common amongst Jews, a "kosher" electric razor, a "magic compass" that points toward Jerusalem, and a method of cutting a diamond into a Jewish star.

Screening for Tay-Sachs Disease with Cloned cDNA for Beta-Hexosaminidase

U.S. Patent Number: 5,217,865

Inventor: Rachel Myerowitz

Date Issued: June 8, 1993

Problem: There are several genetic diseases that occur at a much higher rate in the Jewish community compared to the general population. Tay-Sachs disease is one such disease and about 1 in 30 Ashkenazi (Eastern European) Jews carry a mutated form of the beta hexosaminidase gene leading to about 1 in 3500 newborns having Tay-Sachs. Individuals having Tay-Sachs usually die before the age of four due to the accumulation of gangliosides in the brain's nerve cells. Many Tay-Sachs carriers do not want to marry other Tay-Sachs carriers to prevent the possibility of having a Tay-Sachs child. But how do you know if you are a carrier or if your potential spouse is a carrier?

How the Problem is Solved: In one of the first, if not the first, patent for Tay-Sachs carrier detection, this invention is for a method of preparing a person's DNA to compare it to both the normal and mutated Tay-Sachs version of the beta hexosaminidase gene.

FIG. 3

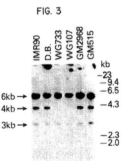

A Shaving Machine

European Patent Number: 2,481,535

Inventor: Itzhak Kataribas

Date Issued: August 1, 2012

Problem: The biggest complaint about electric shavers is that they do not give as close of a shave compared to a razor blade. This is actually the opposite concern for observant Jews because the *Torah* prohibits certain types of cutting around the face. Leviticus 19:27 states, "You shall not round the corners of your heads, neither shalt thou mar the corners of thy beard." There are various interpretations of what this means and how to apply this commandment. Some Jewish sects do not cut the beard at all, while others only prohibit using blades that directly contact the skin. How can an electric razor be made "kosher" so that its use does not violate *halacha*?

How the Problem is Solved: This invention is for an electric razor that has a thicker grid compared to standard electric razors so that the blades never actually contact the skin. The invention is also for a mountable grid to further prevent blades from contacting the skin.

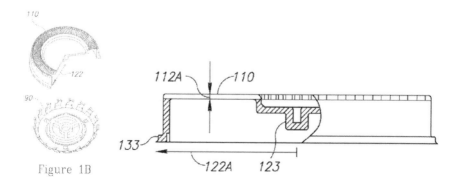

Figure 1B

Magic Compass

U.S. Patent Number: 7,134,213

Inventor: Mark Ashin

Date Issued: November 14, 2006

Problem: Jews are supposed to pray toward Jerusalem. Wouldn't it be nice to have a compass that points toward Jerusalem? But how can this be possible if a compass' needle always points north? You could always figure out where Jerusalem is, relative to north, but wouldn't it be cooler to have a "Magic Compass" that actually points toward Jerusalem?

How the Problem is Solved: This "Magic Compass" can be set to point to any direction by having the actual magnetic compass needle hidden from view under a false bottom. A fake compass needle is connected to the real needle, but angularly offset. While the hidden actual needle points to magnetic north, the fake needle can be set 90° to the right of the hidden needle, so it looks like the compass is pointing east (toward Jerusalem, if you are in America).

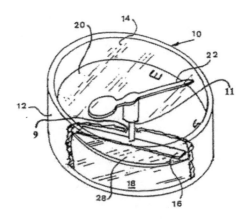

Method for Preparing a Diamond

U.S. Patent Number: 6,591,827

Inventor: Roy Fuchs

Date Issued: July 15, 2003

Problem: Diamonds are cut in my different types of shapes: round, emerald, oval, asscher, marquis, pear, radiant, princess, and heart, just to name a few of the common ones. But what about a Jewish star cut? The Jewish star, called a *Magen David* in Hebrew, is the modern symbol of the Jewish people. How is cutting a diamond into a *Magen David* shape even possible?

How the Problem is Solved: This invention is for a method of preparing a diamond having a six-pointed-star-shaped girdle. The diamond starts off as a round diamond cut, and then six equally sized triangles are cut out to form grooves, shown in the sequence illustrated below.

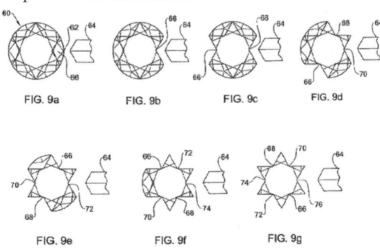

FIG. 9a   FIG. 9b   FIG. 9c   FIG. 9d

FIG. 9e   FIG. 9f   FIG. 9g

Made in the USA
San Bernardino, CA
29 July 2020

76163510R00080